MW01030264

Compass
of Affection

Compass
of Affection

Poems New and Selected

SCOTT CAIRNS

PARACLETE PRESS
BREWSTER, MASSACHUSETTS

Compass of Affection: Poems New and Selected

2006 First Printing

© 2006 by Scott Cairns

ISBN: 1-55725-503-2

    Library of Congress Cataloging-in-Publication Data
Cairns, Scott.
  Compass of affection : poems, new and selected / by Scott
Cairns.
    p. cm.
  ISBN 1-55725-503-2 (alk. paper)
  1. God—Poetry. 2. Theology—Poetry. 3. Christian poetry,
American. I. Title.
  PS3553.A3943C66 2006
  811'.54--dc22
                              2006015105
10 9 8 7 6 5 4 3 2 1

All rights reserved. No portion of this book may be reproduced, stored in an electronic retrieval system, or transmitted in any form or by any means—electronic, mechanical, photocopying, recording, or any other—except for brief quotations in printed reviews, without the prior written permission of the publisher.

Published by Paraclete Press
Brewster, Massachusetts
www.paracletepress.com

Printed in the United States of America

Frontispiece: *The Dormition, after Theophanes the Greek.*

for Marcia, Elizabeth, and Benjamin

Contents

Acknowledgments

The following "New Poems" previously appeared as indicated:
"September 11," *Image: Art, Faith, Mystery*
"In Reference to His Annunciation," *Image: Art, Faith, Mystery*
"Late Sounding," *Image: Art, Faith, Mystery*
"In Hope of Recollection," *Image: Art, Faith, Mystery*
"Euripides the Athenian," *The Paris Review*
"Secret Poem," *The Paris Review*
"Against Justice," *Iron Horse*
"A Prior Despair," *Poetry*
"Two Icons," *Books & Culture*
"Christmas Green," *Books & Culture*
"Narration," *Books & Culture*
  (reprinted in *100 American Poets Against the War*)
"The Righteous Man of Gomorrah," *Mars Hill Review*
"Hidden City," *Spiritus*
  (reprinted in *The Best American Spiritual Writing 2004*)
"Evening Prayer," *Pleiades*
"Replies to the Immediate," *Western Humanities Review*
  (reprinted in *The Best American Spiritual Writing, 2005*)
"Setting Out," *Western Humanities Review*
"Autopsy," *Western Humanities Review*
"Icons," *Tiferet*
"The Leper's Return," *Poems of Francis and Clare*
"Blesséd Being," *Nebraska Review*
"Note," *Lake Effect*
"No Harbor," *Smartish Pace*
"Short Lyrics," *Smartish Pace*
"Bad Theology: A Quiz," *America*
"Brief Age of Wisdom," *The Crossing*
"Trouble," *The Crossing*

I am grateful, as well, to the Research Council of University of Missouri for a research leave during which many of the "New Poems" were completed.

from

The Theology of Doubt

1985

Imperative

The thing to remember is how
tentative all of this really is.
You could wake up dead.

Or the woman you love
could decide you're ugly.
Maybe she'll finally give up
trying to ignore the way
you floss your teeth as you
watch television. All I'm saying
is that there are no sure things here.

I mean, you'll probably wake up alive,
and she'll probably keep putting off
any actual decision about your looks.
Could be she'll be glad your teeth
are so clean. The morning might be
full of all the love and kindness
you need. Just don't go thinking
you deserve any of it.

The Theology of Doubt

I have come to believe this fickleness
of belief is unavoidable. As, for these
back lot trees, the annual loss
of leaves and fruit is unavoidable.
I remember hearing that soft-soap
about faith being given
only to the faithful—mean trick,
if you believe it. This afternoon,
during my walk, which
I have come to believe is good
for me, I noticed one of those
ridiculous leaves hanging
midway up an otherwise naked oak.
The wind did what it could
to bring it down, but the slow
learner continued dancing. Then again,
once, hoping for the last good apple,
I reached among bare branches,
pulling into my hand
an apple too soft for anything
and warm to the touch, fly-blown.

On Slow Learning

If you have ever owned
a tortoise, you already know
how terribly difficult
paper training can be
for some pets.

Even if you get so far
as to instill in your tortoise
the value of achieving the paper,
there remains one obstacle—
your tortoise's intrinsic sloth.

Even a well-intentioned tortoise
may find himself, in his journeys,
to be painfully far from the mark.

Failing, your tortoise may shy away
for weeks within his shell, utterly
ashamed, or looking up with tiny,
wet eyes might offer an honest shrug.
Forgive him.

Taking Off Our Clothes

Let's pretend for now that there is no such thing
as metaphor. You know—waking up will just
be waking up; darkness will no longer have to be
anything but dark; this could all be happening in Kansas.
We could lie back upon a simple bed that is a mattress
at the corner of a floor. We'd have clean, blue
sheets and a wool blanket for later.
I could be the man, and you could be the woman.
We'd talk about real things, casually
and easily taking off our clothes. We would
be naked, and would hold onto each other
a long time, talking, saying things that would make us
grin. We'd laugh off and on, all the time
unconcerned with things like breath, or salty skin,
or the way our gums show when we really smile big.
After a little while, I'd fetch you a glass of water.

The Theology of Delight

Imagine a world, this ridiculous,
tentative bud blooming
in your hand. There in your hand, a world
opening up, stretching, after the image
of your hand. Imagine a field of sheep
grazing, or a single sheep
grazing and wandering in the delight
of grass, of wildflowers
lifting themselves, after their fashion,
to be flowers. Or a woman, lifting her hand
to touch her brow, and the intricacy
of the motion that frees her
to set the flat part of her hand carelessly
to her brow. Once, while walking, I happened
across a woman whose walking had brought her
to a shaded spot near a field. Enjoying
that cool place together, we sat watching sheep
and the wind moving the wildflowers in the field.
As we rose to set out again, our movement
startled the flock into running; they ran
only a little way before settling again
to their blank consideration of the grass.
But one of them continued, its prancing
taking it far into the field where,
free of the others, it leapt for no clear reason,
and set out walking through a gathering
of flowers, parting that grip of flowers with its
face.

Approaching Judea

I am told there are no moose
in Judea; but I have seen them,
thousands and thousands of moose.
                    —Shaya Kline

I've been in this desert longer than I care to
admit to any of you. I haven't eaten a bite
since I left Jerusalem, unless you count the sand
the wind keeps throwing in my face.
I came here for the moose, though everyone
I've asked continues to insist moose
have never been here, and never will be.
I don't care for that kind of talk. I'm convinced
moose can get along anywhere. And where better
than here, a holy land for the holiest of beasts?
I admit, I nearly gave up, girded my sandy loins
for the long walk out. But last night,
I was awakened from my pillow of sand
to a strange calling, a low sound like wind,
but with blood in it. And as I stared blindly
into the blank world, the moon lifted
from behind a dune, lighting up
an entire desert of moose, their shaggy heads
all lifted and calling out their one, holy word.

from

The Translation of Babel
1990

Invitation to a Wedding

Since this is the West, where most borders
approach the quaint artifice
of geometry, so the days themselves achieve
their brief expressions of form.

And likewise, the stuff of days finds some manner
for its gestures: The forms
of greeting, and of play, the sober forms
of worship, the forms love takes

when the mind is rested, the sometimes
astonishing forms of speech.
And then, as in any formal gathering,
the familiar dose of convention—

the cosmetics of the bride and groom,
stiff fabrics to keep the body straight,
flowers to hide the shortfalls of the room,
the wooden orchestrations of our band.

What joy one takes in such square dances
is not so much the familiar steps, more
likely, what lies hidden, or faintly seen—
his false step, her exaggerated spin.

So, as you might accept any public invitation
and chance to overhear the private terms,
you might lift this book from among the others,
this sad and arbitrary book, this book of forms.

Acts

*And how hear we every man
in our own tongue, wherein we were born?*
—Saint Luke, Acts of the Apostles

Memory

The problem with memory is that most
memories are dull; what happens,
in general, is mostly dull. I remember

how dull my own boyhood was, the long wait
for something to happen nearly always
ending in disappointment—Martha Watson's

summer dresses nearly falling away,
but never really falling away.
But suppose one morning without rain she found

her way to my room, the sun entering
with her and lighting up the window
and the bed, lighting her dress as it became

liquid and fell down her arms. I think that
would be interesting. And her high,
small breasts and her strong thighs, lighted up,

would be interesting. I think I would find
everything about her visit
tremendously interesting. That's why even

a little of this extravagance is so
necessary, and why, in the strange
and unlikely light of such visitations,

the apparent nearly always pales into
embarrassment. It's too serious
to want around, too earnest to put up with

for very long; its straight face can
turn laughter bitter in your mouth, choke
the best parts of your past, ruin your life.

Another Morning

Most mornings I wake up slowly. That's just
the way I am. I wake up slow as I can, listening first
to one thing, then another. The milk bottles chiming

just outside the door, then the milk truck idling in the street.
If I'm lucky, the girl through the wall will be singing
and I'll hear her next, singing while she dresses. Maybe

she's brushing her hair, or tying the ribbon for her stocking
—that would be nice. And out in the hall, some man will
probably kiss Miss Weitz good-bye again—yes, I believe

those are their lowered voices now, and that is his cough.
Others are coming out now, their doors opening and closing so
variously, too many to sort out. Why sort them out? And now

the factory whistle is telling the night shift that enough is
            enough.
Now I hear myself humming along, joining in this little chorus
of good intentions. When everything is ready, I'll go out.

Yellow

The town is much larger than you recall,
but you can still recognize the poor.
They vote to lose every chance they get, their faces
carry the tattoo of past embarrassments,

they are altogether too careful. This girl,
here in the print dress, pretending to shop
for an extravagance, the too slow way
her hand lingers between the colors along

the rack, her tentative hold on the clasp—
sure signs she knows she has no business here.
Soon enough she'll go home again with nothing
especially new in her hand. But no one

needs to rush things. The afternoon itself
is unhurried, and the lighted air outside
the store has lilacs in it. Her hand finds
a yellow dress. I think she should try it on.

Infirmities

Some mornings you know you've seen
much of this before.
The kind woman across the street
is lame, and her daughter is lame.

Some defect they've had since birth
is working to dissolve their bones.
The boy three doors down
is blind. And the idiot
girl who sweeps up at the market
insists all day on her own
strange tune. And sometimes they seem
happy enough and sometimes
you might find one alone, muffling
grief with a coat sleeve.

And the shy way the blind boy
laughs when he stumbles
makes you laugh with him some mornings.
Some mornings it hurts to see.

Chore

Of course, what we actually feel is too much
a grab-bag of longing to be anything so simple

as an emotion. What we actually feel could never
be pinned down to a word. My father

was dying, and I was home for a visit.
I did a few chores to help us all get ready.

To speak of how I felt would be a mistake.
I was splitting firewood, loading the woodbox.

It was hard work, and I found some pleasure in it.
I was at the back corner of my father's house,

a place I hadn't seen in years, working easily
and well, my shirt off in the last heat of summer.

Wiping the sweat from my face, I looked up
and saw him, saw that he had been watching me.

We met as well as we could. Behind him a huge jay
bowed a heavy branch. I pointed to the hysterical bird.

Nothing much happened after that. I swung the axe
until I finished the work.

Another Kiss

Far sweeter as a greeting, this parting
of lips became the concluding gesture
love would bear between my father and me.
In this last hour of his death his fever
had retreated so that as my kiss found
the smooth passage of his neck, I felt
how the cold surprise was beginning there.

As so we waited, and I kept my sight
fixed upon his face, which worked with less
conviction—which appeared to acquiesce.
I studied his preference for fainter effort:
the softening of his brow, the rounding
edges and, as if he could speak, the slight
movement of his lips nearly opening.

All of this, so I would remember the hour
and the moment of my father's death,
so I might rehearse the silent language
of this final speech. His lungs were filling
and gave him less and less reason to breathe.
Lifting briefly—his lips in the semblance
of a kiss, and a kiss, a third kiss—he was gone.

After the Last Kiss

By now I'm dead. Make what you will of that.
But granted you are alive, you will need
to be making something more as well. Prayers
have been made, for instance, but (trust me)

the dead are oblivious to such late sessions.
Settle instead for food, common meals of thick soup.
Invite your friends. Make lively conversation
among steaming bowls, lifting heavy spoons.

If there is bread (there really must be bread),
tear it coarsely and hand each guest his share
for intinction in the soup. Something to say?
Say it now. Let the napkins fall and stay.

Kiss each guest when time comes for parting.
They may be embarrassed, caught without wit
or custom. (See them shifting from foot to
foot at the open door?) Could be you will

repeat your farewells a time or two more
than seems fit. But had you not embraced them
at such common departures, prayers will
fall as dry crumbs, nor will they comfort you.

Embalming

You'll need a corpse, your own or someone else's.
You'll need a certain distance; the less you care
about your corpse the better. Light should be
unforgiving, so as to lend a literal
aspect to your project. Flesh should be putty,
each hair of the brows, each lash, a pencil mark.

If the skeleton is intact, its shape may
suggest beginnings of a structure, though even here
modification might occur; heavier
tools are waiting in the drawer, as well as wire,
varied lengths and thicknesses of doweling.
Odd hollows may be filled with bundled towel.

As for the fluids, arrange them on the cart
in a pleasing manner. I prefer we speak
of *ointments*. This notion of one's anointing
will help distract you from a simpler story
of your handiwork. Those people in the parlor
made requests, remember? Don't be concerned.

Whatever this was to them, it is all yours now.
The clay of your creation lies before you,
invites your hand. Becoming anxious? That's good.
You should be a little anxious. You're ready.
Hold the knife as you would a quill, hardly at all.
See that first line before you cross it, and draw.

Leaving Florianopolis

Soon I shall know who I am.
—*Borges, "In Praise of Darkness"*

In Praise of Darkness

Here, behind this attic door is Borges,
waiting in a straight chair, bound there
by thin wire and by rags. Soon you will
ask him the questions again, and soon

he will say his answers, his insane,
his foolish words, smiling as if he had said
enough, as if he had answered what you've asked.
And you will hit him again, and split

his skin; you'll invent pain and slowly
let him know what it is you've made.
But, as before, nothing will have changed.
If he speaks at all he'll only say his

nonsense to the air until you must
hit again to make him stop. So you
come to hate the hand that pulls open
the attic door, that gives you Borges,

waiting in the chair, looking out
from the corner of an attic room.
There is a wash of light from the window, and it warms
his face, his arms; he feels it pouring

through the neat, dark suit he wears.
You believe that he is mad. He is too old
for this and nearly blind, and the light
on his face makes him beautiful.

When you enter the room, he sees
an angel enter; he turns his head
toward your noise, his face expectant.
You have never been so loved.

Lucifer's Epistle to the Fallen

Lucifer, Son of the Morning, Pretty Boy,
Rose Colored Satan of Your Dreams, Good as Gold,
you know, God of this World, Shadow in the Tree.

Gorgeous like you don't know! Me, Sweet Snake, jeweled
like your momma's throat, her trembling wrist. Tender
as my kiss! Angel of Darkness! Angel

of Light! Listen, you might try telling me
your troubles; I promise to do what I can.
Which is plenty. Understand, I can kill

anyone. And if I want, I can pick
a dead man up and make him walk. I can
make him dance. Any dance. Angels don't

get in my way; they know too much.
God, I love theater! But listen, I know
the sorry world He walks you through.

Him! Showboat with the Heavy Thumbs! Pretender
at Creation! Maker of Possibilities!
Please! I know why you keep walking—you're skittish

as sheep, and life isn't easy. Besides,
the truth is bent to keep you dumb to death.
Imagine! The ignorance you're dressed in!

The way you wear it! And His foot tickling
your neck. Don't miss my meaning; I know none
of this is your doing. The game is fixed.

Dishonest, if you ask me. So ask. God
knows how I love you! My Beauty, My Most
Serious Feelings are for you, My Heart turns

upon your happiness, your ultimate
wisdom, the worlds we will share. Me, Lucifer.
How can such a word carry fear? Lucifer,

like love, like song, a lovely music lifting
to the spinning stars! And you, my cooing
pigeons, my darlings, my tender lambs, come, ask

anything, and it will be added to your
account. Nothing will be beyond us;
nothing dares touch my imagining.

Leaving Florianopolis

Carlos I said to myself, which was so
unlike me because my name is not Carlos,

but *Carlos*, I said, *Never fail to do
what is necessary under heaven.*

Good advice, I thought at the time
and think so still. But as necessity

was flourishing so remarkably
well upon departure, I had to lie down.

It was then, opening one eye ever
so slightly, I witnessed the deft flex

of anonymous legs approaching.
These were long and slender and of a hue

a painter in oils would call sienna, use
to limn his garden stalks. I closed my eyes

as she whose dark limbs approached leaned close,
her breath like exotic flowers—all of them blue.

Into the cup of my ear she breathed *Eugene*,
or was it *Raymond*, thinking to wake me

for some device in the hammock. I feigned sleep
and so allowed her whatever game she pleased.

She changed my name many times, but for each
small outrage of the tongue her invention

more than compensated. She wore me so,
I had to feign waking to plead sincere

exhaustion. Listening then to what I took
to be her burnt sienna feet, staccato

across the bright tiles, I dreamed once again
of Florianopolis, that untoward port

whose intriguing flues line the coastal curve
in such alluring designs, and whose women

are forever bidding strangers farewell
with lush gestures—their cool habit of approach,

their lips' blue buds parting, their famous kiss.
Oh, Carlos! How can you leave like this?

Regarding the Monument

But roughly but adequately it can shelter
what is within (which after all
cannot have been intended to be seen).
> —Elizabeth Bishop

Of course it is made of *would*, and *want*,
the threads and piecework of *desire*. Its shape
is various, always changing but always
insufficient, soliciting revision.

> I thought you said it was made of *wood*.
> You said it was made of wood.

Never mind what I may have said; I might
have said anything to bring you this close
to the monument. As far as that goes,
parts of it are wood, parts are less, more.

> Some kind of puzzle? What can it do?
> If the wind lifts again we're in trouble.

Certain of its features endure—its more
sepulchral qualities—whether it gestures
ahead or back, the monument is always
in some sense memorial.

> Is it safe? It looks so unstable.
> Do you think it is safe to come so close?

I don't think it's safe, but I don't think safe matters.
It's changing. Even now. Watch how it turns
into its new form, taking something
of what it was, taking something else.

33

I don't feel well. Does it have to do that?
Is it growing? Still? Something must be wrong.

The monument is growing still, even if
diminishment must be a frequent stage
of its progress. If we return tomorrow
it may appear much less; it may seem gone.

I don't see the point. What is the point?
I'm leaving now; you stay if you want.

But the part that lies buried, its foundation,
will forge its machinery ever and again,
and the wind will return it to motion,
if more powerfully, and more horribly.

The Translation of Raimundo Luz

I show you a mystery: we shall not all sleep,
but we shall all be changed.
—Saint Paul to the Corinthians

Note: Raimundo Luz is the greatest postmodern poet writing in
Portuguese. He has never left his birthplace, Florianopolis, Brazil.
His father was a mender of fishing nets, his mother, a saloon
singer. He has no formal education, having gathered all he knows
from books. He reads seven modern languages, also ancient Hebrew,
ancient Greek, and Latin. Luz is best known as a radical theologian,
identifying himself paradoxically as a Christian-Marxist. He is a
devoted family man, a fan of American rhythm and blues, an
accomplished cook, and a fiction.

The Translation of Raimundo Luz

1. My Infancy

How like a child I was! So small and so
willing! And the world was extravagant

and beyond reach even then. All those lovely
apparitions flitting close, and then away—

I loved them. Even their inconstancy.
God was always tapping his curious

music in my head. I'm sure I seemed aloof,
but the opposite was true—such a pleasant

distraction, so good! this music of God,
his calming voice. Wonderful odors

everywhere—these dark, human odors.
Sometimes I would taste them. And the salt

of mother's breast, yes, and then that sweet milk
of dreams, dreams and appalling distance.

2. My Personal History

Mother bore me without pain.
Something of a miracle I'd say.
Father never doubted my love.

My brother was my better self.
All these frail poems
—beloved sisters.

Good fortune everywhere.
Grace, abundant and wet on our faces.
Exotic fruits plentiful as grass.
God still humming his engaging lyric
in my each. Air?
Tender, sweet cake.

Just out the door—a jungle.
Just out the door—a blue sea.
And always between waking
and sleep, this marvelous
confusion of a jungle and a sea.

And later, so many beautiful
women to marry.
They all cared for me.
I married the most generous.

We have a daughter
who resembles me,
but so prettily.
A great miracle.
One morning we three
slept luxuriously in the same bed.
In her drowse, the baby nursed.
God loves Raimundo.
I woke first.

3. My Language

Portuguese is my language,
and that is appropriate.
That is as it should be.

A language somewhat akin
to Spanish, but with ironic
possibilities as well. A perfect
language for my purposes.
One does not weep in Portuguese.

Can you hear its music? Its
intelligent distance? (No, of course not.
You are not reading Portuguese now.)

The boats in the harbor are rapt
in conversation with the sea.
The air sings high Portuguese.

When I was a boy, I nearly learned
German too. A narrow escape.
I am careful to avoid things German,
in particular the food. As for English,
I leave that now to whoever needs it.
I never look north from Florianopolis.

Here, I have everything I need: a generous woman,
this daughter, my garden, Portuguese.

4. My Mortal Dream

In which I am driving through what I presume
to be a northamerican city. I have never seen
a northamerican city, but I think this one is St. Louis.
It is not a very clean city, even the air has fingerprints.
Windows of the huge tenements are without glass.
The few people I catch sight of are sleepwalking.

At the signal I stop my car, which I believe
is a Volkswagen. I wait for the light and examine
my surroundings. A man with a gun is taking money
from a station attendant. He counts the bills
and shoots the man, who then seems a boy, and now
a sack of leaves. The criminal lifts his face to mine
and I nod. He points. I turn to face the light. The window
explodes in my ear, and my life begins.

5. My Imitation

I sold my possessions, even the colorful pencils.
I gave all my money to the dull. I gave my poverty
to the president. I became a child again, naked
and relatively innocent. I let the president have my guilt.

I found a virgin and asked her to be my mother.
She held me very sweetly.

I watched father build beautiful shapes with wood.
He too had a gentle way.

I made conversation in holy places with the chosen.
Their theater was grim.

I suggested they cheer up. Many repented,
albeit elaborately.

I floated the wide river on a raft.
I set Jim free.

I revised every word.

One morning, very early, I was taken by brutes and beaten.
I was nailed to a cross so sturdy I thought
father himself might have shaped it.

I gestured for a cool drink and was mocked.
I took on the sins of the world and regretted my extravagance.
I gave up and died. I descended into hell
and spoke briefly with the president.

I rose again, bloodless and feeling pretty good.

I forgave everything.

6. Our Lost Angels

Ages ago, clouds brought them near
        and rain brought them to our lips.
        They swam in every vase, every cupped palm,
        We took them into ourselves
        and were refreshed.

For those luckier generations, angels
        were the sweet, quickening substance
        in all light, all water, every morsel of food.

Until the day the sun changed some, as it had,
    took them skyward, but thereafter
    the clouds failed to restore them.
In time, streams gave up
    every spirit, and the sea, unreplenished,
    finally became the void we had feared
    it would become, the void we had imagined.
And, as now, clouds brought only rain,
    and the emptied rain
    brought only the chill in which
    we must now be wrapped.

7. Embarrassment

The witness caught Raimundo's drift and looked away.
A stale taste dried his open mouth.

The girl in the upper room dressed the ancient doll.
The witness spat, began to pout.

Raimundo shrugs and scribbles on a yellow pad.
The problem's not so simple. Stick around.

8. My Goodness

I have such good intentions.
I have enormous sympathy.
I am aware of a number
of obligations.
In the Hebrew, Enoch
walked with God and was no more.
A difficult translation,
but so intriguing!

I am a little skeptical,
but nonetheless intrigued.
How far must one walk
in such cases?

I suppose I shouldn't tell you,
but I have suspected something
like this. I have had an inkling.
Call it a hunch.

Even so, I manage so little faith.
My goodness is deficient.
I walk for days and looking up
bump again into my own closed door.

9. My Denial

Such a very long night. So demanding
of one's better judgment. I was alone.

Or I seemed alone. My friends had all left
on earlier trains. The raised platform

I paced was poorly lit, my train not due
for another hour. Then the stranger came.

He walked past me once, then turned, surprised;
his appearance—either frightened or insane.

He pronounced a name—certainly foreign—
asked if we hadn't perhaps met before.

If he was familiar, it was nothing
more than a resemblance to any chance

acquaintance. I told him no, he was mistaken.
The wind came up like a howl. He left me.

From behind my book I watched him settle in
at the platform's farthest end. I checked the time—

my train still far away. Then, the soldiers came,
maybe a dozen soldiers. They appeared

suddenly and from every passage.
They came to me rudely, demanded my name.

I told them my business. I was waiting
for a train. Their captain pointed to the stranger

at the platform's end and asked me
if I knew the man. No, I said, I am only

waiting for a train. They dropped me and fled
to the other's bench. They slapped him awake,

picked him up by his coatfront and began
dragging him my way. As they pushed past,

I asked what he had done. The captain stopped,
asked why I had to know. Was I his friend?

No, I said, I've never seen him before tonight.
don't know the man at all. Take him.

10. My Good Luck

Fortunately, there are mitigating circumstances.
Fortunately, Raimundo doesn't get what he deserves.
Confronted by embarrassment, I lift my bed and walk.

The comfort lies in fingering the incoherent for the true.
The comfort lies in suspecting more than evidence allows.
My only rule: If I understand something, it's no mystery.

As you might suppose, I miss my father very much,
and if I think of his dying, I can become deeply sad.
Giving yourself to appearances can do a lot of harm.

So I remember the morning my father died, and the ache
of his relief, the odd, uncanny joy, which began then
and which returns unbidden, undeserved, mercifully.

11. My Amusing Despair

I confess that I am not
a modern man. As a modern man
I am a little flawed.
Raimundo is far too happy.

Many times, more times
than I would care to admit to you,
I have suffered from this
unforgivable lack, this absence.

All around me, poets
tearing at their bright blouses, tearing
at their own bare flesh.
All night long—their tortured singing.

And still I have suffered
an acute lack of despair. Why is that?
Is Raimundo stupid?
Am I unfeeling? Doesn't the bleak

45

weight of the north ever
pinch my shoulders? Well, no, not often.
And when it does—which is
not very often—I can't help feeling

a little detached. As if I had
somewhere else to go. As if
I were a spectator,
a dayworker watching the slow clock.

I have an interest in the outcome,
but not a strong interest.

12. My Farewell

Things are happening. Daily,
I come across new disturbances
in my routine. I am curiously
unsettled. I dress myself
and the clothes fall to the floor.
I scratch my head. Dust
in my hand. All morning
arranging flowers, and for what?
Petals fallen, litter
on the pretty cloth. I march
straightway to the mirror
and shake my fist. My hand
is a blue maraca scattering petals.
I shout my rage and hear
my words praising the vast
goodness of the world. This
is beyond my control.
Even so, I am slowly learning one thing;
of one thing I am slowly becoming

aware: whether or not I would
have it so, whether I sleep
or no, I will be changed.
I am changing as I speak. Bless you all.
Suffer the children. Finished. Keep.

from
Figures for the Ghost
1994

The Holy Ghost

Don't worry about it. Other figures would serve as well,
so long as they too imply the sort of appalling stasis
which still provokes unseen, albeit suspected, motion:
a murmur caught in the throat, heart's stammer, vertigo.

A windmill! Now *that's* lucky. But only if the rope is
secure which holds the lead blade to the anchor,
only if, against the fiercest gale, the blades cannot turn,
though they tremble, though they threaten even to come crashing

down, or to be torn away—perhaps spinning now
and deadly—to some murderous reunion with the earth.
Well, that's a little theatrical, but you see what I mean.
The issue is the flight one's mind provides while influenced

by that shuddering stillness making itself . . . what? Supposed?
There were so many distractions along that narrow bay,
so many nearly invisible coves you would not find
unless your boat was slow enough to let you trace the seam.

My fortune was the little coracle I had occasion
to row across the inlet. In retrospect, the chore
appears habitual, as if whole seasons had been measured
by my pulling against my grip on the chirping oars,

watching my wake's dissolution, its twin arms opening
to a retreating shore. And, true enough, I may have crossed
that rolling gulf many times each day in fair weather. Still,
I suspect this part I remember best happened only once:

I am rowing steadily enough, davening across
that bay and reaching the choppy center where I pause,
ostensibly to rest. But the breeze also stops, and a calm
settles upon those waters so suddenly I worry

for my breath, and can hardly take it in. And I am struck
by a fear so complete it seems a pleasure,
and I know if I were to look about—though I know better
than to try—I would find the circle of shoreline gone,

and myself adrift in an expanse of stillest waters.
Well, it didn't last. A little air got in, and I sucked it up,
and the boat lifted, almost rocking, across a passing swell.
The shoreline was called back to its place, its familiar shape,

and there were people on it, and I think a couple dogs.
So I kept rowing, though I wouldn't remember until
I'd docked the boat why I'd made the trip. It was an errand
to call my brother back from swimming, which I did.

Return Directive

Back out of all this now too much for us . . .

The road there—if you take the road and not
the shorter, crude diagonal that cuts
across a ruined and trampled pastureland—
is nearly winding as a spiral stair.

Wind there neither flags nor any longer
rages as a fabled wind might have done;
the winding road grants progressive, hidden
groves where you might find sitting still

a profitable diversion from what
journey you thought to take, and each of these
may disclose a path or two—game trails,
but I think more than game might find some use

in taking one. Such a path I'm guessing
may never bring you back, but will demand
another turn, in turn, another choice,
and you will choose and walk, choose and pause.

If lost at all you're lost to those behind you;
to what's ahead you're a kind of imminence.
Besides, whatever loss or gain the others
measure, you will know what line you travel

and, if you live and move, how far, how well you fare.

Prospect of the Interior

A little daunting, these periodic
incursions into what is, after all,
merely suspected territory.

One can determine nothing from the low
and, I'm afraid, compromised perspective
of the ship, save that the greenery is thick,

and that the shoreline is, in the insufficient
light of morning and evening, frequently
obscured by an unsettling layer of mist.

If there are inhabitants, they've chosen
not to show themselves. Either they fear us,
or they prefer ambush to open threat.

We'd not approach the interior at all
except for recurrent, nagging doubts
about the seaworthiness of our craft.

So, as a matter of course, necessity
mothers us into taking stock of our
provisions, setting out in trembling parties

of one, trusting the current, the leaky
coracle, the allocated oar.

The Glass Man

He is the transparence of the place in which He is . . .

This is where he washed to shore
during rough weather in November.
We found him in a nest of kelp,

salt bladders, other sea wrack—
all but invisible through
that lavish debris—and we might

have passed him by altogether
had he not held so perfectly
still, composed, so incoherently

fixed among the general
blowziness of the pile.
Unlikely is what he was,

what he remains—brilliant,
immutable, and of speech
quite incapable, if revealing

nonetheless. Under foot,
the landscape grows acute, so that it seems
to tremble, thereafter to dissolve,

thereafter to deliver to the witness
a suspicion of the roiling
confusion which brought him here.

Serenade

The Past? I held it only briefly, but it was mine.
Evenings with the past were best of all: so much
of the day behind us,

so little left, she would undress by candlelight
(we all had candles then; I'm talking about The Past),
and she was pleased to stand

a long while before me—too long, really—accepting
my eye and the warm swelling of the room, savoring
the wonder of her flesh,

its momentary, astonishing colors pulsing.
Then, the bedclothes, the ribbon at her thigh, the fire
of each trembling candle,

the murmuring of what seemed music in my throat—
all wavering as she like a wave opened
over me and we met.

That was the gift of The Past to me, earlier
version—less elaborate, less mediated
life—but a version without

which I could not be: fragrant oil of The Past, ache
and arc of a reflected radiance, umber
flame coloring our selves.

The Death of Penelope

She went, as you would guess, in her famous,
perversely faithful bed, alone, longing
for her lost boy (wandering desperately
God knows where) her absent daughter (hostage
to a petty, hostile man, by all accounts
incapable of gratitude for what
little luck he onetime must have held)
and longing, if only a little less,
for the hero, long estranged and never
heard from after parting for "one last journey"
to plant an oar in some flat wilderness.
One supposes the clever man must have run
clean through his gamut of tricks, and run out
of stories too, perhaps, as he lay face down
in a stony, treeless field, far from home,
his vast holdings, but approaching the deep,
unpleasant laughter of the inside
oracular joke, witnessing the dissolve
of all topography, finding against
his face the grinning abyss, himself
unable to let go the little oar.

But as the woman lay dying, for whom
the many-passaged myth was always
her own story, as she lay tasting this new,
sudden pain, which took each harshest, prior
trial and made of each a mere cordial
leading to this full draught of bitterness,
just as she glanced about, about to find
herself finally overrun with sorrows,
she found across the room's pure air her loom,

emptied of work, bright with erasure,
bearing only the nothing that suggests,
in its blank face, an approaching visage,
in its stillness, a note rising, as she
fully consumed by pain also rises,
imagines she stares back reading her long
tale of vacancies, pattern of absence,
and constructs of these a new, a stranger
story, now commencing. As the faithless
body and its weakness for toleration
fall finally to the misshapen tree,
Penelope rises, lets fall her dress,
begins the journey, nothing in her hands.

for P.A.

Advent

Well, it *was* beginning to look a lot like Christmas—everywhere, children eyeing the bright lights and colorful goods, traffic a good deal worse than usual, and most adults in view looking a little puzzled, blinking their eyes against the assault of stammering bulbs and public displays of goodwill. We were *all* embarrassed, frankly, the haves *and* the have-nots—all of us aware something had gone far wrong with an entire season, something had eluded us. And, well, it was *strenuous*, trying to recall what it was that had charmed us so, back when we were much smaller and more oblivious than not concerning the weather, mass marketing, the insufficiently hidden faces behind those white beards and other jolly gear. And there was something else: a general diminishment whose symptoms included the *X*s in Xmas, shortened tempers, and the aggressive abandon with which most celebrants seemed to push their shiny cars about. All of this seemed to accumulate like wet snow, or like the fog with which our habitual inversion tried to choke us, or to blank us out altogether, so that, of a given night, all that appeared over the mess we had made of the season was what might be described as a nearly obscured radiance, just visible through the gauze, either the moon disguised by a winter veil, or some lost star—isolated, distant, sadly dismissing of us, and of all our expertly managed scene.

City Under Construction

As you might suppose, the work was endless. Even when at last the City stood gleaming like flame in the troubled radiance of that distended sun, we could not help but be drawn to where our next project should begin: The loosening bolt, flaking surfaces, another unnerving vibration in the yawning superstructure.

We made a joke of it: The Eternal City! And let our lives run out reworking the old failures, refining our materials, updating techniques, but always playing catch-up to a construction that just wouldn't hold, fretwork that wouldn't stay put, girders complaining under the accumulating matter of successive generations and an unrelenting wind.

Granted, it could have been worse; at least the work served as an emblem of perpetual promise as every flagging strut commenced another stretch of unquestioned purpose—mornings when we rose from our beds eager and awake, thoroughly enjoyed our food, and hurried out to work.

Nor would it serve to slight the rich pathos we shared like a warming drink with co-workers. For there we'd be—touching up the paint or turning the heavy wrench for the hundredth time—and we'd smile, shake our heads theatrically, say to each other how our City was *insatiable*.

Just the same, this was not precisely what we had intended—that our City should grow into a self-perpetuating chore. Earlier, we had imagined—more or less naively—a different sort of progress, one with a splendid outcome. We fancied a final . . . conclusion, from which we would not be inclined to retreat.

I recall how, long before we had so much as made a start, before we had cleared the first acre or drawn the first plan, we saw the City, and as near completion then as it would ever be, infinite in the best sense, its airy stone reaching to the very horizon, and—I think this is the issue—extending invisibly past.

The History of My Late Progress

First, what you might call the odd shoe dropping:
the mid-life (well, not—it turns out—*mid*-life)
heart attack, not massive by clinical
standards, but a close call what with fumbling
technicians, a rough ride to emergency.
I thought I was a goner.
                                    Not really.
No one, I guess, ever really thinks that.
The closest we come is this uncanny,
dispassionate sitting-back, just watching
to see how we'll be saved. And then I was.
It was hard work for all of us, and hard
work for me thereafter,
                                 tasting the new
bitterness—that any of this could end.
My somatic recovery advanced
passably. I agreed to medication,
certain and acceptable restrictions:
diet, activity, and so on.
I agreed to continue
                       as if I'd gained
new enthusiasm for simple things
like fishing, breathing, looking around.
Still, I'd been struck—apparently mid-stride—
by a little surprise. As *that* chagrin
faded, as the dose of bitterness sank
from memory,
                     I recalled something else.
Dying (even if I hadn't *died*, I'd
been *dying*) had an unexpected slant.
I mean, granted, I had watched those doctors,

62

their assistants, caught up, extravagant
in their procedures—each of them of *huge*
interest—
          but I was interesting too.
Oddly unafraid. Troubled, but eager.
It is my eagerness *then* which troubles
me *now*, the exotic thought that I was
more than just willing to see what would come.
Still, recovery is never complete,
which is just as well.
                    And in recent years—
the interim—other developments:
diabetes, The Big C (here, then there),
heart surgery. Each brought about its own, extreme
demands, new chores, graceless dispensations.
Finally, one's late sentiments catch up
to what the body has
                    long determined.
Time. Time out. There has been labor here; one
prefers to imagine there is a style
of progress even after . . . after here.
So, with the merest supposition, I
proposed to recover something I had
lost, had relinquished,
                    now just suspected,
and in my so far severed circumstances
found agreeable, vast, beckoning.

The Beginning of the World

In the midst of His long and silent observation of eternal presence, during which He, now and again, would find His own attention spiraling in that abysmal soup, God draws up what He will call His voice from unfathomable slumber where it lay in that great, sepulchral Throat and out from Him, in what would thereafter be witnessed as a gesture of pouring, falls the Word, as a bright, translucent gem among primal turbulence, still spinning. Think this is evening? Well, that was night. And born into that turmoil so bright or so dark as to render all points moot, God's pronouncement and first measure.

But before even that original issue, first utterance of our Great Solitary, His self-demarcation of Himself, before even that first birth I suspect an inclination. In God's center, something of a murmur, pre-verbal, pre-phenomenal, perhaps nothing more disturbing to the moment than a silent clearing of the hollowed throat, an approach merely, but it was a beginning earlier than the one we had supposed, and a willingness for something standing out apart from Him, if nonetheless His own.

Still, by the time anything so weakly theatrical as that has occurred, already so many invisible preparations: God's general availability, His brooding peckishness, an appetite and predilection—even before invention—to invent, to give vent, an all but unsuspected longing for desire followed by the eventual arrival of desire's deep hum, its thrumming escalation and upward flight into the dome's aperture, already open and voluble and without warning giving voice.

But how long, and without benefit of Time's secretarial skills, had that Visage lain facing our direction? What hunger must have built before the first repast? And, we might well ask, to what end, if any?

And if any end, why begin? (The imagination's tedious mimesis of the sea.) In the incommensurate cathedral of Himself, what stillness?

What extreme expression could prevail against that self-same weight? And would such, then, be approximate to trinity? An organization, say, like this: The Enormity, Its Aspirations, Its Voice. Forever God and the mind of God in wordless discourse until that first polarity divests a shout against the void. Perhaps it is that first resounding measure which lays foundation for every flowing utterance to come. It would appear to us, I suppose, as a chaos of waters—and everything since proceeding from the merest drop of it.

So long as we have come this far, we may as well continue onto God's initial venture, His first concession at that locus out of time when He invented the absence of Himself, which first retraction avails for all the cosmos and for us. In the very midst of His unending wholeness He withdraws, and a portion of what He was He abdicates. We may suppose our entire aberration to proceed from that dislocated Hand, and may suppose the terror we suspect—which lingers if only to discourage too long an entertainment—to be trace and resonance of that self-inflicted wound.

So why the vertiginous kiss of waters? Why the pouring chaos at our beginning, which charges all that scene with . . . would you call it *rapture*? Perhaps the dawning impulse of our creation, meager as it may have been, pronounced—in terms we never heard—God's return.

Dead Sea Bathers

What stillness their hearts must know, these bathers
laid out and glistening along the dissolve
of an ancient sea,

their bodies—so late from brief exercise,
so lately thrown down in exhaustion—
already marbled

with a fine, white dust as they stretch across
straw pallets arranged by unseen servants
who, one supposes,

must see what we see. And how calm their thoughts,
these still brilliant shapes, as the mind's ebbing,
the heart's slow measure

lull the vessel and its oils, which now retard
to an all but breathless pace akin
to idiocy,

if saved by just that by the hum of faint
discomfort, that murmur beginning deep
as the flesh is fired.

Disciplinary Treatises

1. On the Holy Spirit

If, upon taking up this or any scripture,
or upon lifting your one good eye to inspect
the faintly green expanse of field already
putting forth its late winter gauze of grasses,

you come to suspect a hushed conversation
already underway, you may also find sufficient
grounds to suspect that difficult disposition
we call the Ghost, river or thread drawn through us,

which, rippled as any taut rope might be, lifts
or drops us as if riding a wave, and which fends
off, for brief duration, our dense encumberment
—the flesh and its confusions—if not completely,

if only enough that the burden be felt and savored,
just shy of crushing us.

2. The Embarrassment of Last Things

Already you smile, drop your eyes, and chew your cheek.
Centuries of dire prophecy have taught us all
to be, well, unconvinced. And there have been decades,
entire scores of years when, to be frank, wholesale

destruction didn't sound so bad, considering.
You remember, we were *all* disappointed.
That the world never ended meant we had to get
out of bed after all, swallow another dose

of stale breath with our coffee, scrape the grim ice
from our windshields one more time. On the way to work,
stuck in endless traffic, the radio or some
incredibly sincere billboard would promise us again

an end to this, and for a moment we almost
see it. But we know it's not an end, not really;
it's harder than that—some kind of strenuous chore
stretching out ahead like these stalled cars, showing our

general direction, inadvertently or not mocking our pace.

3. *Sacraments*

Doubtless, Grace is involved—when is it not?—but its
locus is uncertain, remains the cardinal
catch whenever we dare interrogate again
our sacramental dogma. After all, Grace may

lie, contracted, inaccessible in Yahweh's
ancient vault, and it could be these painstakingly
enacted tokens of mystery are really
about as good as paper money. But what if

even the troubled air we breathe were drenched above
our knowing with the golden balm of Adonai?
Well, I like to get carried away. Never mind
the wearied questions of which and how many

dear rituals may qualify, the dire attributes
of divine participation are what these days
could stand some specifics, or, say, a little more
dogmatic elucidation. For it may be

some dreadful portion—very God of very God—
makes periodic and discreet returns, piecemeal,
sabbatical visitation to a matter
and a territory otherwise absenced to suffer

our mutual and—let's face it—flagging venture.
But who knows? The Holy may flourish any form
figuring the self's diminishment,
any conjunctive ebbing that yields a reply.

4. The Communion of the Body

> The Christ in his own heart is weaker
> than the Christ in the word of his brother.
> —Bonhoeffer

Scattered, petulant, argumentative,
the diverse members generally find
little, nothing of their own, to offer

one another. Like us all, the saved
need saving mostly from themselves, and so
they make progress, if at all, by dying

to what they can, acquiescing to this
new pressure, new wind, new breath that would fill
them with something better than their own

good intentions. Or schemes of community.
Or their few articulate innovations
in dogma. What the Ghost expects of them

is a purer than customary will
to speak together, a *mere* willingness
to hear expressed in the fragmentary

figures of one another's speech the mute
and palpable identity they share,
scoured clear of impediment and glare,

the uncanny evidence that here
in the stillest air between them the One
we call the Ghost insinuates his care

for the unexpected word now fondling
the tongue, now falling here, incredible
confession—that they would be believers,

who startle to suspect among the scraps
of Babel's gritty artifacts one stone,
irreducible fossil, capable

of bearing love's unprovoked inscription
in the locus of its term.

5. Angels

As with wine, one might tender an entire lifetime
with hierarchies and their array of habits,

characteristic chores, nearness to the Holy,
their special tricks. One might speculate their number.

And what has not been said about these our brothers?
So little of it reliable, so little

corresponding to the actual, to the pure
indifference with which most angels skim aloft

our understanding, either incapable
of seeing our distress, or not interested.

Still, stories—never verifiable—persist:
the fortunate warning, the inexplicable swerve.

These insinuate themselves against our better
judgment, provide comfort beyond apparent cause.

There are other stories, after all, more somber
accounts of angelic intercourse: How, by force

of guile, a woman or a boy has been taken, made
an unwilling portal for some monstrosity

or one of many lies. This version I believe.
Angels are of two sorts; best not to provoke either.

6. *Satan*

And while we're on the subject of angels—
their dubious character, their famous
unreliability—we should pause

to examine the notorious, one-
time hero and major disappointment:
The Bright One, Chief Ingrate of the Most High,

Morning Star, Petty Prince, *et cetera.*
Say what you dare, he still *is* somebody.
And, if ever I could open my eyes

sufficiently to see what the air is
full of, I might be torn by his glory
even now, even as it is—rebuked,

diminished, scoured raw unto an extreme
radiance, and I daresay I'd find my
knees, and cower there, and worship him, which

action would gain me a measure of his part.

7. Baptism

Of those first waters in which we rolled and swam oblivious and
from which we fled into this confusion of life and death, here is a
little picture. Granted the scheme has undergone some modest
accommodation for the sake of decorum, practicality, and—who
knows?—our unwillingness to risk a chill, so that the symbolic
return to Christ's dire tableau is, well, less than obvious, and one
might subsequently risk infusing the elements themselves with a
little magic. No real harm there, probably, unless one is then disin-
clined to appreciate a metaphor when it's poured in his face.

In the older way, then, the trembling primitive would be led into a
river where he would likely hear some familiar business about his
being buried, whereupon he would go under. What each receives at
this point—underwater—is fairly individual, pretty various, unlikely
to be written down. But then he is returned and, surfacing, hears
that he is raised in the likeness of a resurrection. He swims in
such affusions as he regains the littered shore.

8. Blood Atonement

This much we might say with some assurance:
a crucifixion occurred, apparently

gratuitous, but a harsh intersection—
tree and flesh and some iron. We might add
that sufficient blood resulted to bring about
a death, the nature of which we still puzzle.

As to why? Why the blood? Why the puzzle?
It seems that no one who knows is saying,
which is not to say we lack opinion.

Still, while we suffer no shortage of dire
speculation, hardly any of it
has given us anything like a clue.

All we dare is that it was necessary,
that we have somehow become both culprit   ·
and beneficiary, and that we

are left to something quite like a response
to that still lost blood, to the blameless world.

9. *Grace*

Long before you knew desire, Desire turned
to you, saw you as you are even now—
unlovely, a little embarrassed, dead.

Can you remember the throat's pure pulse first
waking you to a longing you could neither
fix to a name, nor satisfy?

Probably not. But it must have happened.
For thereafter under the influence
of Desire's instruction, you made desire

the new light by which you would dare proceed,
and it has led you here, where you adopt
the drape of love's body and find your own.

10. A Recuperation of Sin

I suppose we might do away with words like *sin*.
They are at least archaic, not to mention rude,
and late generations have been pretty well schooled

against the presumption of holding *anything*
to be absolutely so, universally
applicable, especially anything like

sin, which is, to put it more neatly, unpleasant,
not the sort of thing one brings up. Besides, so much
of what ignorance may have once attributed

to *sin* has been more justly shown to be the end
result of bad information, genetic flaw,
or, most often, an honest misunderstanding.

And I suppose sin's old usefulness may have paled
somewhat through many centuries of overuse
by corrupt clergy pointing fingers, by faithless

men and women who have longed more than anything
for a more rigid tyranny over their wives
and husbands, over their somnambulant children.

In fact, we could probably forget the idea
of *sin* altogether if it were not for those
periodic eruptions one is quite likely

to picture in the papers, or on the TV—
troubling episodes in which, inexplicably,
some giddy power rises up to occasion

once more the spectacle of the innocents' blood.

11. Pain

No new attempt at apology here:
All suffer, though few suffer anything
like what they deserve.

Still, there are the famous undeserving
whose pain astonishes even the most
unflinching disciples

whose own days have been consumed by hopeless
explanation for that innocent whose torn
face or weeping burns

or ravenous disease says simply no,
not good enough. This is where we must begin:
incommensurate

pain, nothing you can hope to finger
into exposition, nothing you can
cover up. A fault

—unacceptable and broad as life—gapes
at your feet, and the thin soil you stand
upon is giving way.

12. *The End of Heaven and the End of Hell*

At long last the feeble fretwork tumbles
apart forever and you stand alone,
unprotected, undeceived, in fullness.
And we are all there as well, equally

alone and equally full of . . .Ourselves.
Yes, I believe Ourselves is what we then
become, though what *that* is must surprise
each trembling figure; and in horror

or elation the effect will be the same
humility, one of two discrete sorts,
perhaps, but genuine humility.
And that long record of our choices—your

every choice—is itself the final
body, the eternal dress. And, of course,
there extends before us finally a measure
we can recognize. We see His Face

and see ourselves, and flee. And shame—old
familiar—will sustain that flight unchecked,
or the Ghost, forgotten just now—merest
spark at the center—will flare, bid us turn

and flame unto a last consuming light:
His light, our light, caught at last together
as a single brilliance, extravagant,
compounding awful glories as we burn.

From the Father

—qui ex Patre

As you might expect, my momentary vision barely
qualifies: you know, sensation something like the merest
swoon, some uncertainty about why all of a sudden
the back garden, its bamboo and rose, the reaching pecans
(one's apparent field contracting to a field of vision)
took to trembling, as well as other accompanying
uncanniness. I mean, *was* the garden trembling or had
it suddenly, unnaturally stopped? Was the disturbing
motion something I was seeing or something I was
seeing with? And why am I asking you?

Perhaps I'm not. Probably, the most I'm doing is one
kind of homage to a moment and a form, a rhetoric
disclaiming what the habitual senses can't make much of.
This is what I can vouch for: I was at rest in a still,
restful corner of our back garden. I had expected
even to doze, but instead found my attention fixing
all the more alertly on the narrow scene, and then I
wasn't seeing anything at all, which is why I'm less
than eager to call this business exactly a vision.
Does one ever sink into a vision?

Let's suppose one might. Once interred, what does one come to find?
I found the semblance of a swoon, and began to suspect
ongoing trouble at the heart, a fullness in the throat,
an expanding, treble note whose voice was neither mine alone
nor completely separate. I know enough to know you
cannot believe this, not if I were carelessly intent
on saying it was so. It was a fiction which I chanced

upon as evening overtook our walled back garden—
whether by virtue of light's ebbing or the fortunate
influx of approaching shade, who would say?

Mortuary Art

Even the ancient, open gate—whose hinges may
as well be stone, whose purpose has always been
purely ornamental—rests extravagantly
at its protected terminus: black *fleurs-de-lys*
topping a Byzantine blaze of black ironwork.

Once you've entered, the live-oak- and ash-dappled expanse
of gaudy statuary seems infinite, spreads
far as you can see and, presumably, farther:
a great many winged forms, more or less angelic,
some bearing human burdens, others extending

arms in an open embrace, but all with the same
expressionless faces of weary dockworkers.
Whichever narrow lane you choose, you find ahead
a multitude of crosses: Latin mostly, but
mingled with scores of Greek and Celtic, one or two

Pattée, Botonée, and down a lonely detour
the still, dire flames of one startling, spiny Maltese.
Pausing before any one of these explains
what time is for: lending weather its circumstance
for dissolving whatever it happens across.

All cemetery roads converge upon a center
where—dwarfed and nearly obscured by outsized,
marble masonry and a high ring of ancient
trees (so much like stone)—lies a brackish pool like tar.
Nothing lives in it: its waters compose a grim

accumulation of poisons laid out to keep
the foreground neat, deceptively green, natural.
Still, one is very likely to neglect the font
(so easy it's become to slight what isn't blemished),
and wander off, though the dust of the throat goes drier.

From the shallows of that ruined pool, a copper tube
—flanged at the lip, and no thicker than your finger—
blossoms out beyond its stem into something
of a calyx, or white anemone, a wavering
rush of water so pure you'll want to drink of it.

One imagines we need not confuse the fountain
with its pool any more than we need pretend
the gate, the angels, the scores of crosses partake
in our little stroll among the dead, or suffer
interest in our being here among them.

In that cove, water from the font leaps up, its foam
drawing light from some obscurity beyond the trees,
inviting all who have come this far to proceed
a little farther, to press their lips against
the rising pulse where all may drink or may withdraw.

from
Philokalia
2002

Late Results

We wanted to confess our sins but there were no takers.
—Milosz

And the few willing to listen demanded that we confess on television.
So we kept our sins to ourselves, and they became less troubling.

The halt and the lame arranged to have their hips replaced.
Lepers coated their sores with a neutral foundation, avoided strong
    light.

The hungry ate at grand buffets and grew huge, though they remained
    hungry.
Prisoners became indistinguishable from the few who visited them.

Widows remarried and became strangers to their kin.
The orphans finally grew up and learned to fend for themselves.

Even the prophets suspected they were mad, and kept their mouths
    shut.
Only the poor—who are with us always—only they continued in the
    hope.

Descents

Dive down into your self,
and there you will find the steps
by which you might ascend.
—Saint Isaac the Syrian

A Lot

A little loam and topsoil
is a lot.
    —Heather McHugh

A *vacant* lot, maybe, but even such lit vacancy
as interstate motels announce can look, well, pretty
damned inviting after a long day's drive, especially
if the day has been oppressed by manic truckers, detours,
endless road construction. And *this* poorly measured
semi-rectangle, projected and plotted with the familiar
little flags upon a spread of neglected *terra firma,*
also offers brief apprehension, which—let's face it,
whether pleasing or encumbered by anxiety—dwells
luxuriously in potential. Me? Well, I *like*
a little space between shopping malls, and while this one may
never come to be much of a garden, once we rip
the old tires from the brambles and bag the trash, we might
just glimpse the lot we meant, the lot we hoped to find.

Poetics for Two

In the exclusive schema of her syntax,
my presence was assumed. Despite the many

obvious advantages of *that*, my own
desires—and you can probably guess them—

went largely unconsidered, and my preference
for promising obscurities—the thin or less thin

veil, the mediating margin introduced
by contrasting shades of rough or fragile

fabric—passed unexamined. The negligée
was frequently neglected altogether,

which made for pure appearances—true enough—
but overlooked the subtler advantages

bound in well-taught cloth. Whatever gain
accessibility enjoyed also served

to deny the more complicated play
of certain tedious labors. Her arms

upraised as she reclined were ample
invitation even so to dismiss the fancy's

solitary musing and partake.

Blesséd

By their very designations, we know the meek
are available for all manner of insult,
the poor have no effectual recourse against
the blithe designs of the rich, and that enigmatic
crew we recognize as merciful still refuses
to stand up for itself, which makes of them all prime
objects for whatever device the brutes ordain.
In time, they become mute relics for those who mourn.
If any still crave righteousness, they are maligned,
then stuffed with straw and burned, or hacked to bits and burned.
If the pure are anywhere present, we wouldn't
know them, which is surely to their advantage. And those
who would make peace are jailed in adjoining cells, simply
dismissed from any arena that matters now.

Promise

Someone is to come, is now to come.
                    —*Derrida*

"When the Messiah comes," we mumble as we pore
over our knotted and confused translation. Should
we listen we may hear with a blush that begins
in the breast and rises, and seems even to reach
the responsive leaves of the fringe tree overhead.

The responsive leaves of the fringe tree overhead
fly back as if breathed upon, but that is surely due
to the first gust of the gathering storm approaching,
so we are not inclined to make much more of their
quick flight than that, though we may wince under the *new*

compunction—the common failure to make more. How
often and how clearly must we say these words
before we finally hear them, and their weight reveals
what mute hope they must have harbored all along,
and without our notice, which we only now set down?

Possible Answers to Prayer

Your petitions—though they continue to bear
just the one signature—have been duly recorded.
Your anxieties—despite their constant,

relatively narrow scope and inadvertent
entertainment value—nonetheless serve
to bring your person vividly to mind.

Your repentance—all but obscured beneath
a burgeoning, yellow fog of frankly more
conspicuous resentment—is sufficient.

Your intermittent concern for the sick,
the suffering, the needy poor is sometimes
recognizable to me, if not to them.

Your angers, your zeal, your lipsmackingly
righteous indignation toward the many
whose habits and sympathies offend you—

these must burn away before you'll apprehend
how near I am, with what fervor I adore
precisely these, the several who rouse your passion.

The Spiteful Jesus

Not the one whose courtesy
and kiss unsought are nonetheless
bestowed. Instead, the largely
more familiar blasphemy
borne to us in the little boat
that first cracked rock at Plymouth
—petty, plainly man-inflected
demi-god established as a club
with which our paling generations
might be beaten to a bland consistency.

He is angry. He is just. And while
he may have died for us,
it was not gladly. The way
his prophets talk, you'd think
the whole affair had left him
queerly out of sorts, unspeakably
indignant, more than a little
needy, and quick to dish out
just deserts. I saw him when,
as a boy in church, I first
met souls in hell. I made him
for a corrupt, corrupting fiction when
my own father (mortal that he was)
forgave me everything, unasked.

Adventures in New Testament Greek: *Metanoia*

Repentance, to be sure,
but of a species far
less likely to oblige
sheepish repetition.

Repentance, you'll observe,
glibly bears the bent
of thought revisited,
and mind's familiar stamp

—a quaint, half-hearted
doubleness that couples
all compunction with a pledge
of recurrent screw-up.

The heart's *metanoia*,
on the other hand, turns
without regret, turns not
so much *away*, as *toward*,

as if the slow pilgrim
has been surprised to find
that sin is not so bad
as it is a waste of time.

Hesychia

Stillness occurs with the shedding of thoughts.
                    —Saint John Klimakos

Of course the mind is more often a roar,
within whose din one is hard pressed to hear
so much as a single word clearly. Prayer?

Not likely. Unless you concede the blur
of confused, compelled, competing desire
the mind brings forth in the posture of prayer.

So, I found myself typically torn,
if lately delivered, brow to the floor,
pressing as far as I could into prayer,

pressing beneath or beyond the roar
that had so long served only to wear
away all good intentions, baffling prayer.

Polished hardwood proves its own kind of mirror,
revealing little, but bringing one near
the margin where one hopes to find prayer—

though even one's weeping is mostly obscured
by the very fact and effect of one's tears,
which, for the time being, must serve.

Adventures in New Testament Greek: *Hairesis*

Surely ours would prove a far less tedious faith
all around if even a few among the more
zealous, more conspicuous brethren knew enough

to make a good heretic or two. My own glib
trespasses are clear enough, but when we're talking
heresy, I'd like to think I'm siding with the angels.

Hairesis finds its home in *choice*, in having chosen
one likely story over its more well received counterpart,
whose form—to the heretic—looks far

less compelling. Poor Arius aside, most heretics
have borne their chosen isolation with something like
integrity, and have spoken to *The Good* as well

as they could manage. Most have spoken quite as well
as they could see. And it's not as if any of us
ever had anything like an adequate view.

The benediction I would choose would be the one
invoking *all* the names of God, Who by all
accounts I'm buying spans the gamut,

as well as everything between each slight,
as well as everything beyond. Historically—
which really has to be the toughest

circumstance in which to figure Him—supposition
hasn't always met with sympathy. No,
you don't need me to underscore the poor

reply with which the body has from time
to time addressed its more imaginative
members, but I would admit what shame

we share, allowing pettiness and fear
to acquire the faint patina of a virtue,
butchery, an ecclesiastical excuse.

Does one always *make* one's choices? From what
universal view of utter clarity
might one proceed? Let me know when you have it.

Even heretics love God, and burn
convinced that He will love them too.
Whatever choice, I think that they have failed

to err sufficiently to witness less
than appalling welcome when—just beyond
the sear of that ecstatic blush—they turn.

Shore View, with Fog

The roaring alongside he takes for granted,
and that every so often the world is bound to shake
—Elizabeth Bishop

Half of what I see seems patently compliant,
while half denies nearly altogether every
pointed query of the eye. The fog (more strangely,

this quality of leaden light the fog affords)
extends to all debris here at my feet a new,
an unaccustomed vividness—the layered,

pale yellow sand, the pink and rust and coal-black stones,
this tattered sea-wrack ribbon stretching traced
from here to (think of it) clean around our ragged,

bristling continent. Retraced, every day! And twice!
While half (that would be the first half, mind you) stretches
quite presentably, the balance (which I suppose

the better half) abides beyond the frame. Which is
a shame, given that the eye pores nonetheless
determined, pokes all the more intently under

every half-apparent surface lolling near our
littered shore. Quite a chore—I'm suddenly convinced—
to navigate a gulf whose every gull and piper

thrives on blind, ecstatic flight. Just now a good half
dozen skirt the sheet suspended underneath
their similarly spry and glazed reflections, which

they seem to kiss, repeatedly—an affectionate,
albeit culinary dip to parse the grit
or seafoam, whose every ebb and fall can slow so . . . well,

seductively the pulse. Whatever animating
bits they siphon from the sand must satisfy
intensely—given how they hurry, how they stare.

Conversely, even as I speak, I can't quite shake
vague dissatisfaction as I walk, keep walking,
continue missing half.

The Modern Poets

had first to supply as fitting complement
to the plow, the loft, the timid flock an urban
avatar or two, had first to raise the City's
patent mediocrities to roughly Orphic
tenor, even such gross vehicles as Coupes DeVille
and Packards. They had thereafter to endow
with prophetic agency such proximate folk
as sausage vendors, the ubiquitous barkers
of burlesque, the jaundiced hacks. More delicate yet,
if they would succeed our moderns would need resist
as well the wince or smirk regarding all of the above
as lesser vestige of the bygone Bucolic scape.

In this, most would fail, albeit famously,
but a few—and you can probably name them—
would observe among the City's earnest
indigenes and bright machinery an immanence
they would not greet embarrassed, but would esteem.
Upon the span, the tug, among the legion
mazing passages and thriving scenes, these
would entertain a vivid host of angels,
if not quite unawares, would receive as dew the kiss
of sleet, as the murmur of bees the hived drone
of the rain wet El, as incense an idling exhaust.

Three Descents

1. Aeneas

As the belovéd Palinúrus sank
more deeply beneath wave and memory,
as the remnant of his race descended

painted planks to step on foreign shore
and there spark fire, gather wood and water,
even as the god's red fist fell hard into the sea,

Aeneas pressed through tangled underbrush
to gain the door to hell. First, of course, he found
the temple of another petty god, graved

with images of all that lay ahead—
his fortune and the fate of every soul
he'd implicated in his flight from Troy.

He barely looked, so used he had become
to how little pleasure Time could bring,
so engaged by the prospect of stepping

briefly out of it, if only to return
to Time's demands when he returned to light.
He hurried through the golden vault to find *her*

whose words would lead him through the awful gates.
And what would he remember years from now
of what he'd find? Little, save the wretched

figure of his own father coupling death,
nearly indistinguishable amid
that mass of shades like dogs tied together

whining. And the figure of the Sybil
likewise bound, then tossed, a bent toy skipped across
a marble floor, moot refusal widening

her eyes, opening her throat as the god's thin voice
coughed out the infernal terms Aeneas
believed he sought, might welcome, until he heard them.

2. *Orpheus*

That his eyes positively shone with the image
he had shaped—of sweet reprieve, of his hand upon
the belovéd, lifting her from the narrow crypt

caught floating on barren stillness, unaccustomed
silence—could not be comprehended by those few
whose minds retained a trace of how the present gloom

was nothing of itself but served to amplify
the absence of the luminous occasions worked
above. That his lit gaze upon those shades who lined

the path could hurt them like a flame did not occur
to him, though he observed their trembling as he passed,
had puzzled as they shrank, slipped back into the Dis.

Her tender heel bitten to the bone, the woman
could barely walk the ruined path she followed down,
and as he pressed with greater speed to apprehend

her frail figure hobbled by its crumbling clay, she turned
to understand the source of sudden suffering,
as if a boy had held a surgeon's glass above

a shriveling midge now stricken by the sun's light drawn
and focused to a beam. As their eyes met, her loss
was total and immediate. When he returned

alone to the sunlit world of things, his life
became one long attempt at shaking free his culpability
in her undoing. And later, as his own flesh

was torn, his body sundered by the famished hands
of famished women, he breathed a last, a single note,
contrite at how his lesser love had hurt her.

3. Jesus

That his several wounds continued to express
a bright result, that still the sanguine flow
coursed tincturing the creases of his cheek

and wended as he walked to bless the bleak,
plutonic path with crimson script declaring
just how grave the way that he had come,

that underfoot the very clay he traveled
sank beneath an unaccustomed weight
occurs as no surprise. That he was glad

is largely otherwise, as would be the news
that every sprawling figure found *en route*
acquired at his approach an aspect far

more limpid than the lot that lay ahead.
As if his passing gained for hell itself
a vivifying agency, each shade

along the way rose startled, blinking, at once
aware that each had been, until this moment,
languishing, until this moment, dead.

Thus, suddenly aware that each among
the withered crowd had by his presence met
a sudden quickening, the multitude

made glad by his descent inclined to join
him on the path recovering each loss,
exulting in each past made newly present.

His etched face luminous and very flesh
made brilliant by the unremitting pulse,
he gains the farthest reaches where the ache

of our most ancient absence lay. He lifts
our mother and our father from beneath
the mindless river, draws them to himself, and turns.

Adventures in New Testament Greek: *Nous*

You could almost think the word synonymous
with *mind*, given our so far narrow
history, and the excessive esteem

in which we have been led to hold what is,
in this case, our rightly designated
nervous systems. Little wonder then

that some presume the mind itself both part
and parcel of the person, the very seat
of soul and, lately, crucible for a host

of chemical incentives—combinations
of which can pretty much answer for most
of our habits and for our affections.

When even the handy lexicon cannot
quite place the *nous* as anything beyond
one rustic ancestor of reason, you might

be satisfied to trouble the odd term
no further—and so would fail to find
your way to it, most fruitful faculty

untried. Dormant in its roaring cave,
the heart's intellective aptitude grows dim,
unless you find a way to wake it. So,

let's try something, even now. Even as
you tend these lines, attend for a moment
to your breath as you draw it in: regard

the breath's cool descent, a stream from mouth
to throat to the furnace of the heart.

Observe that queer, cool confluence of breath

and blood, and do your thinking there.

Having Descended to the Heart

Once you have grown used to the incessant
prayer the pulse insists upon, and once
that throbbing din grows less diverting

if undiminished, you'll surely want
to look around—which is when you'll likely
apprehend that you can't see a thing.

Terror sometimes sports an *up* side, this time
serves as tender, hauling you to port.
What's most apparent in the dark is how

the heart's embrace, if manifestly
intermittent, is really quite
reliable, and very nearly bides

as if another sought to join you there.

Recitation

He did not fall then, blind upon a road,
nor did his lifelong palsy disappear.
He heard no voice, save the familiar,

ceaseless, self-interrogation
of the sore perplexed. The kettle steamed
and whistled. A heavy truck downshifted

near the square. He heard a child calling,
and heard a mourning dove intone its one
dull call. For all of that, his wits remained

quite dim. He breathed and spoke the words he read.
If what had been long dead then came alive,
that resurrection was by all appearances

metaphorical. The miracle arrived
without display. He held a book, and as he read
he found the very thing he'd sought. Just that.

A life with little hurt but one, the lucky gift
of a raveled book, a kettle slow to heat,
and time enough therefore to lift the book

and find in one slight passage the very wish
he dared not ask aloud, until, that is,
he spoke the words he read.

Eventual City

I am of the opinion that He is going to manifest some wonderful outcome, a matter of immense and ineffable compassion.
—Saint Isaac the Syrian

Eventual City

—like Venice, save
that the canals are scarlet, and decay

impossible, neither are the boats
subject to fatigue, neither are the boatmen

whose broad alae suggest great patience.
Its pure stone rises, immaculate—and new

construction will not impede adjacent
progress. If the bearing of those going on

about their work seems fixed, intent, it is
nonetheless benevolent. The air also

broods, scented, though not so as to cloy.
And rather than paling flesh, the light

extends to it a vivid carnality.
The city is nothing at all like Venice,

what made me think it was? Something—maybe
something atemporal in the pulse, or else

the cool painterly quality the eye
attains during its mute pause at the pier.

Or it could be my confusion underscores
a blurred range of effects the body wakens

under the initial blush of just such gravity
attended by an also unfamiliar readiness.

Ruminant

When he reads, let him seek
for savor, not science.
　　　—Arnoul of Bohériss

So that was why the monk's thin lips
trembled as he took the holy fruit—
how *every* word becomes a subtle
flesh whose savor one infers piecemeal
as he . . . ruminates. Near enough.
Swallowing whole is fine for dogs,
but even cattle mark the latent good
of mulling matter over and again
—if never quite *again*, given
that the apparent, local matter
of a word will always promise
in its telling textures to be more
the sort of gum whose sugars will
not quit, nor ever quite hold still.

Adventures in New Testament Greek: *Mysterion*

What our habit has obtained for us appears
a somewhat meager view of mystery.
And Latinate equivalents have fared
no better tendering the palpable
proximity of dense noetic pressure.

More familiar, glib, and gnostic bullshit
aside, the loss the body suffers when
sacrament is pared into a tidy
picture postcard of absent circumstance
starves the matter to a moot result, no?

Mysterion is of a piece, enormous
enough to span the reach of what we see
and what we don't. The problem at the heart
of metaphor is how neatly it breaks down
to *this* and *that*. Imagine one that held

entirely across the play of image
and its likenesses. *Mysterion* is
never elsewhere, ever looms, indivisible
and *here*, and compasses a journey one
assumes as it is tendered on a spoon.

Receiving it, you apprehend how near
the Holy bides. You cannot know how far.

As We See

The transfiguration of our Lord—that is, the radiance in which
he was bathed at the pinnacle of Mount Tabor—did not manifest
a change in Him, but a change in those who saw Him.
                                               —Isaac the Least

Suppose the Holy One Whose Face We Seek
is not so much invisible as we
are ill-equipped to apprehend His grave
proximity. Suppose our fixed attention
serves mostly to make evident the gap
dividing what is seen and what is here.

The Book there on the stand proves arduous
to open, entombed as it is in layers
of accretion, layers of gloss applied
to varied purposes, hardly any of them
laudable, so many, guarded ploys
to keep the terms quite still, predictable.

Which is why I'm drawn to—why I love—the way
the rabbis teach. I love the way they read—opening
The Book with reverence for what
they've found before, joy for what lies waiting.
I love the Word's ability to rise again
from chronic homiletic burial.

Say the One is not so hidden as we
are kept by our own conjuncture blinking,
puzzled, leaning in without result. Let's say
the meek, the poor, the merciful *all*
suspect His hand despite the evidence.
As for those rarest folk, the pure in heart?
Intent on what they touch, they see Him now.

Formal Brief: The Name

Forgive my having recourse just above
to the legalistic idiom. Forgive
my having chosen to pursue a measured
argument—and in such lax verse. Forgive
as well my penchant for ironic tone,
for all my insufficiencies—those few
committed here, the many others, there.

And now that you are thus inclined, extend
the courtesy to those who likewise don't
deserve it. Address the water in the pool
and leaning in forgive yourself. The Name
won't bear repeating—I dare say—without
such kind provision. Even so, The Name
will bear thereafter subtle fruit suffused

beyond our reckoning, which also serves
as sweet inducement to repeat The Name.
Some among the saints have found in time
their prayer avails most palpably in silence,
and some have found a path from mind to heart.
Regarding such, I may have more to say
in future, but let's not hold our breaths.

My own rough habit has led to my preferring
to invoke The Name aloud, to draw its shape
into my mouth, to bring together breath
and tongue, to feel those syllables proceed
as tremor to the port of trembling air,
to hear my own voice colored by The Name,
to taste and see—and *then* to savor silence.

Once Called, Thereafter

. . . spirited from sleep, the astounded soul
Hangs for a moment bodiless and simple. . . .
*   —Richard Wilbur*

The suspense is familiar, not likely to last,
but wakens the soul to how fit, how meet remain
the body's modest properties reposed.

The yellow flower—as it happened—became far
more yellow with the sun's approach and, when *that* fire
first cleared the eastern ridge, poured its light

upon our clearing, upon the thousand golden
stalks, blessed their yellow flower with a yellow light,
it proved a yellow deeper than the eye.

Called back at dawn to their accustomed coupling, both
the ghost and her abundant paramour are pleased
to sustain these kind affections, and proceed

upon the morning as one new, impossible
creature bearing bright burnishments of limb and frame,
bearing also in that flesh its quickening.

Adventures in New Testament Greek: *Apocatastasis*

Among obscurer heresies, this dearest rests
within a special class of gross immoderation,
the heart of which reveals what proves these days to be
a refreshing degree of filial regard.

Specifically, the word is how we apprehend
one giddy, largely Syriac belief that all
and everyone will be redeemed—or, more nearly,
have been redeemed, always, have only to notice.

You may have marked by now how late Semitic habits
are seldom quite so neighborly, but this ancient one
looks so downright cordial I shouldn't be surprised
if it proved genesis for the numbing vision

Abba Isaac Luria glimpsed in his spinning
permutations of The Word: Namely, everything
we know as well as everything we don't in all
creation came to be in that brief, abysmal

vacuum The Holy One first opened in Himself.
So it's not so far a stretch from *that* Divine Excess
to advocate the sacred possibility
that in some final, graceful *metanoia* He

will mend that ancient wound completely, and for all.

Memento

In some circles, skulls still serve as graphic
and conventional choice, especially
when what one hopes to call to mind is *Death's*
indisputable if typically discounted
imminence. Here, in the artist's study,
even this diminutive Golgotha underhand
can serve as scene for just such fraught locality,

as evidenced by a good dozen such paintings,
famous ones, a spate of lyric, plastic,
and dramatic works, not to mention quite a run
of recurrent nightmare billings. One
particularly agéd practice of the ancient Church
promotes actual discourse with the dead;
we speak of them as if they now might hear us,

and we speak *to* them as if they might care
—and more than that, might speak in our behalf.
The icons of the several saints I love the most
create a vivid gallery—if one in that word's
rarer sense, wherein the blessed reposed within its arc
are the crew in best position to comprehend
the view. These surround the shallow altar

where I say my prayers and, if I'm lucky,
where I pray. When I say my prayers, of course,
there is much to remember; when I begin to pray,
far more to forget. In any event, we visit the dead,
and *that* tilt of the head thereafter avails
a curious space, wherein we conceive that we too
rest among them—seated maybe, communing

certainly, though afterwards who can recall
exactly what was shared? I can't imagine
that anything was actually said, even if
in that silent vault they nonetheless seemed to speak.
Each brief visit remains about as enigmatic
as you'd guess—a vivid tableau upon which I
might still gaze, but surely irreducible

to paraphrase. Every altar in our churches bears
a holy fragment—bit of bone, most often—
as testament to the uncommon and genuine
honor in which we hold the body—even
shattered bits of it, even when its habitant has,
for all appearances, gone hence. Each mute relic
serves as token both of death *and* of life's appalling

ubiquity—even there. It helps to bear in mind
the curious and irreparable harm the Crucified
inflicted upon the nether realm when graved
He filled it with Himself, and in so doing, burst
its meager hold and burst its hold on us—*all*
of which has made the memory of death lately
less grim. *Gehenna* is empty, and tenders

these days an empty threat. Remember that.

Sacred Time

Not time at all, really, but space
like you don't know, and knowledge there,
in general, finally admits

how meager a consolation
it has been all along. Once
you grow accustomed to the sprawl

and velocity your own mind
articulates (and that queasy
rocking tapers to a hum) you might

have pause to entertain a sense
of presence reaching suddenly,
and now, and deeply, ever so.

New Poems

2006

Blessèd Being

So few poor among us save   the actual poor, who acquire
in due time a serene dis-   interest regarding whatever
evil tomorrow may bring.   So few among us quite willing
to adopt that poverty   promising to adorn the heart
in efficacious tatter.   And so our being yet looms large
if largely out of reach, yet   retains the tremor troubling
the evening's dim diffusions   enhanced just now by scotch
                                                      served neat.

Where was I? And where was I   prepared to go? Honest, I'd hoped
by now to have accomplished   a somewhat more reliable
demeanor. I'd hoped by now   to have commenced, at least, to pray.
One day, I hope to do so   free of the incredulous,
glib, incessant columnist   established in his box seat, beaming.
How might one dip beneath that   murmur, descend into a self
unadorned, undistracted,   wholly present to the Blessèd

Being in Whom another   blessed being comes to be?

Narration

This is the abomination. This is the wrath. . . .
—W.H. Auden, *For the Time Being*

If, on account of the political situation, the press
has become an increasingly incredible source
of quite palpable frustration, if certain
of our neighbors have been made objects
of suspicion, or have become, themselves,
both irritable and suspicious, if our leaders
address their glib monologues with relative success
to the conspicuously inattentive, if the language
of the tribe has been reduced to far fewer syllables,
and the eyes of the tribe tend to glaze over at the first sign
of a subordinate clause, that is our due. We have long
desired that our confusions abate, regardless.

If certain travelers are now subject to untoward
scrutiny, if their baggage, clothing, and orifices are all
equally fair game, if the poor of other lands fail to figure
in the calculus of the launch, and if our own poor
alternate between suicidal rage and suicidal obesity,
if the water carries a taste of tin, and our daily bread
contagion, these too are just deserts. And yes,
the pattern established by our lately narrower range
of variables has attained the look and the feel of permanence.

We have voted, and have agreed not to suffer
the impractical illusions of an earlier time. Who can blame us?
Who would dare? If we prefer the spoiled child's temper
to actual courage, prefer the pride of the cock to anything
smacking of humility, if we prefer what we call justice
to the demands of mercy, what is that to you?

The kingdom has come. We appear quite taken with it.
For the time being, God's will has acquiesced to our own, at least
in this, the kingdom of anxiety, the only realm we care to know.

Brief Age of Wisdom

Its beginning was the day embarrassment
sat you down, hard, banging your knees against
the tiny desk, the day all your answers—
though good as any—were not good enough.

Stunned as Mr. Reichmann aimed his finger
at your heart, you finally caught his curt demands
for compliance, blithe conviction concerning certain
established tables—multiplication?

periodic? Fictions unambiguous,
and fixed, constructions of self-evident
importance—but far beyond you, apart
from you, your playmates, the girl you addressed

from a distance during recess. Yes, somewhat
clearer now. First taste of a compelling
humility that might have led somewhere,
this suspicion, this beginning and last chance.

Trouble

Easy enough to ignore in the glare
of daylight's demanding distractions, chores
which comprise the care, feeding, general
hosing down of our children, the stooping,
clearing of decks, the specific, endless
pinching from the carpet the scraps, debris,
baffling residue of life with children.

But when they finally descend (and so
abruptly) into their disturbingly deep
drowse, when the house is about as tidy
as it will ever be so long as they
live in it, when suddenly you are caught
standing in the middle of the dim room,
surprised to find nothing in your hands . . .

Bad Theology: A Quiz

And lo, the angel of the Lord came upon them,
and the glory of the Lord shone round about them:
and they were sore afraid.

Whenever we aver "the God is nigh,"
do we imply that He is ever otherwise?

When, in scripture, God's "anger" is said
to be aroused, just how do you take that?

If—whether now or in the fullness—we
stipulate that God is all in all, just where

or how would you position Hell? Which
is better—to break the law and soothe

the wounded neighbor, or to keep the law
and cause the neighbor pain? Do you mean it?

If another sins, what is that to you?
When the sinful suffer publicly, do you

find secret comfort in their grief, or will
you also weep? They are surely grieving;

are you weeping now? Assuming *sin* is *sin*,
whose do you condemn? Who is judge? Who

will feed the lambs? The sheep? Who, the goats?
Who will sell and give? Who will be denied?

Whose image haunts the mirror? And why
are you still here? What exactly do you hope

to become? When will you begin?

Setting Out

Pilgrim: What is it that you do here?
Monk: We fall, and we get up again.

In time, even the slowest pilgrim might
articulate a turn. Given time enough,

the slowest pilgrim—even he—might
register some small measure of belated

progress. The road was, more or less, less
compelling than the hut, but as the benefit

of time allowed the hut's distractions to attain
a vaguely musty scent, and all the novel

knickknacks to acquire a fine veneer of bone-
white dust, the road became then somewhat more

attractive, and as the weather made a timely
if quite brief concession, the pilgrim took this all

to be an open invitation to set out.

Against Justice

Do not say that God is just; His justice
is not in evidence in His dealings with you.
                    Saint Isaac of Syria

As the day is storm-begotten, so its luminous effects
attain a frankly horrifying face, and every burst arrives
accompanied by rain so sharp it bites the pilgrim's back,
and drives him helplessly away from what has passed for home.
What has passed for home recedes along a washed-out bed
whose bank has over time acquired a grim array—particulate
debris and silt, the scattered wrack that might yet bear a body's

pause, a body's mute reflection. But chalk all that to weather,
and to the sure erosion of the road, and to the chore
of passing on, of suffering the trek from here to there. It's all
a little wild, and all a little slow, and everything
takes on the feel of slightly arbitrary choice, and not just
a little pointless. I'd felt that much of this had more to do
with circumstance, and to the pilgrim's sometimes solipsistic bent,

than to the necessary wage of anxious undertaking.
Yes, I know the poem is difficult, but far more likely to be read
than any script the habits score. The chore, as I've suggested,
lies in tracing any solid thread between the outcome
and its cause, any lead, or leading proposition posed
so as to offer what might pass for revelation. The God
is hardly just, and we are grateful for His oversight.

Two Icons

I. Nativity

As you lean in, you'll surely apprehend
the tiny God is wrapped
in something more than swaddle. The God

is tightly bound within
His blesséd mother's gaze—her face declares
that *she* is rapt by what

she holds, beholds, reclines beholden to.
She cups His perfect head
and kisses Him, that even here the radiant

compass of affection
is announced, that even here our several
histories converge and slip,

just briefly, out of time. Which is much of what
an icon works as well,
and this one offers up a broad array

of separate narratives
whose temporal relations quite miss the point,
or meet there. Regardless,

one blithe shepherd offers music to the flock,
and—just behind him—there
he is again, and sore afraid, attended

by a trembling companion
and addressed by Gabriel. Across the ridge,
three wise men spur three horses

towards a star, and bowing at the icon's
nearest edge, these same three
yet adore the seated One whose mother serves

as throne. Meantime, stumped,
the kindly Abba Joseph ruminates,
receiving consolation

from an attentive dog whose master may
yet prove to be a holy
messenger disguised as fool. Overhead,

the famous star is all
but out of sight by now; yet, even so,
it aims a single ray

directing our slow pilgrims to the core
where all the journeys meet,
appalling crux and hallowed cave and womb,

where crouched among these other
lowing cattle at their trough, our travelers
receive that creatured air, and pray.

II. Dormition

Most blessed among all women and among
the mass of humankind,
in this fraught image our mother is asleep.

She lies arms crossed and, notably, across
the spacious foreground
upon an altared bed, her head upraised

upon a scarlet robe,
and we surround her strange repose perplexed
by grief that couples homage

nonetheless. Not we, exactly, but our holy
antecedents, whose bright
nimbi gleam undimmed despite their weeping.

Here again the icon serves
to limn the artifice of time, drawing
to this one still point a broad

synaxis of the blessed, including some
whose souls unbodied have
preceded her to Paradise. Most are bent

in sorrow; several raise a hand to meet
fresh tears. They mourn the dire
severing of blessèd soul from blessèd body.

Leaning in, Saint Peter
lifts the censer with a prayer. Saint Andrew
nearly falls upon the bier.

Saint James Alpheus looks away, or looks
for solace to Saint Luke,
whose eyes—like those of Saints Heirtheus

and adjacent brother James—
direct us to the cupola behind our grief,
from which the risen Christ

attends the mother's solemn funeral
even as he bears her
gleaming spirit in his arms, where she,

so meek the weeping pilgrim might have missed her,
rests swaddled in her shroud,
waiting to be borne to Him, and bodily.

Christmas Green

Just now the earth recalls His stunning visitation. Now
the earth and scattered habitants attend to what is possible: that He
of a morning entered this, our meagered circumstance, and so
relit the fuse igniting life in them, igniting life in all the dim
surround. And look, the earth adopts a kindly áffect. Look,
we almost see our long estrangement from it overcome.
The air is scented with the prayer of pines, the earth is softened
for our brief embrace, the fuse continues bearing to all elements
a curative despite the grave, and here within our winter this,
the rising pulse, bears still the promise of our quickening.

A Prior Despair
—after Kavafy

When I saw that I had lost her   completely, I sought the dulcet
taste of her on the lips of each   subsequent woman, her fragrant
flesh in the fold of every lover's   nape thereafter, and her heat
welling with my own and drawing   out an urgency in each
ambiguous woman met   in that tortured interim.

When I saw that I had lost her   I was lost, and held
my eyes shut tight that I might so   delude my wits as to trust
that it was she receiving me,   that it was she returning
with delight the urgent drive   against the unbearable
distance—two bodies, struggling   toward agreeable repose.

Then, tasting once a sudden kiss   so suddenly presented,
I saw another prospect rise   to view, and knew reprieve
from the familiar ring of hell,   from which I rose and marveled
at the offer of another life   whose heat and heady fragrance
rose, delirious to burn   deliciously, and not consume.

Short Lyrics
—after Seferis

Turning Point

When the stillness (sent
by what hand?) finally
settled here in my breast
as a mute, black dove, or

as a coal, glowing
without color or light,
and the road opened
before me, and the crust

of bread in my mouth
softened with that wine, you,
stillness I have desired,
woke me, deeply.

Slowly

Before the sun, you spoke
as darkness hovering
pressed our embrace
into something more

than embrace, and even
now, I remember
the sensation like a taste,
a vague ache.

Where is it now, that
savor and moment
when our common breath
drew these thirsts together?

Her Sorrow

Upon the flat stone, longsuffering,
she sits awaiting evening,
the black coals of her eyes
radiating grief (do you feel it?)

her lips a scarlet line,
naked and (do you see?) trembling
as her soul dizzies, her entire
body sobs one plea,

her mind the well, inexhaustible,
from which her tears
draw hot supply, though she
had so nearly turned again,

but her sorrow, thus embraced,
becomes what fills
the night's expanse
with (see them?) so many eyes.

Carriage

Down the rush of road and open
to each intersection's parting
of the way—the wind caressing the hair,
the miles filling our bellies—

we two fled, emptying, frantic
for affection—the mind's áffect, the blood's,
both failing, leaving us exposed,
and each a sparking nerve.

. . . *drawn together, once, in bed, the pillow*
raised and airy, the scent
of our confusion, and all separateness
slipping away into its bleak sea . . .

Dim, forgetful, we slogged
along our separate roads,
parting, unaware, dis-
embodied, thick with isolation.

Late Denial

In the secret cove,
sands white as dove-down,
we parched, and the water
was useless—half salt, half sweet.

On evening's gilded, ruddy sand,
we etched her name,
but the sea-wind rose
and the script was taken elsewhere.

With what wild craving, hot breath,
what lush ecstasies we pursued
our union there—apparent error.
Chagrined we turned away.

Companions in Hades
> *. . . but he deprived them of the day of their return.*
> —*Odyssey*

We ignored our meet provisions—
fools that we are, and faithless—
and disembarked to partake
of what was available and slow,

consuming in haste
and thoughtlessly the elements
we might have honored, and by
so doing, honorably won.

Surrounded by life we swallowed
death. We gorged on it,
and settled in these dim regions,
regardless, grinning, full.

Late Apocalypse

And I turned to see the voice that spake with me.
And being turned, I saw…

Blessed is anyone who reads much of anything, blessed
and most unusual. And blessed be the one who gleans
from any text or texture of the latter day a word
of prophecy. As for they who keep those things
they read, they are abundantly blessed and of very
little consequence. The world—impossible conceit—
dwindles in its substance even as its matter flourishes,
and those who might direct it otherwise would be the last
to jimmy up the works that keep them fed and keep
their pampered offspring buffed and quite oblivious
to the evil they perform, the evil they rely upon.
And we, the *remnant ineffectual*, fare hardly better, being
chagrined and silenced by effusive ignorance our own
kind yammers, and choking back our rage at the blithe
demeanor of the opposition. I turned and saw before me
seven bright convenience stores, each laden with a hoard
of sugars and of oils, fuels devised by economics to obtain
the most satisfaction with the least actual good. I turned
and saw before me seven military vehicles in black
and red and yellow, each driven by an unattractive man
or a highly polished woman. I turned and saw before me
seven Wal-Marts in a row, and, lo, flowing in and out their doors
a multitude—likened unto apes, corpulent, unhealthy apes,
circus animals towing their young, slapping them every seven
steps or so, schooling them in how they too might one day
bequeath such systematic self-destruction as a sole inheritance.
I turned and beheld seven rows of plasma screens, each bearing
seven vivid scenes, each flickering, each pulsing with a light
revealing distant terrors, conflagrations, sufferings—and all

thereby brought so close, and all thereby kept far away.
I did not turn, but heard from behind a voice like a golden horn
assuring that the image and the sound would prove of highest quality.

The Leper's Return
—a gift of Saint Francis

He had grown used to the fear he brought
to every soul he passed along the road,
though the chagrin he bore inside became

a bitterness worse than the fetid taste
that never left his mouth. He could not bear
to stay near town for long, nor could he yet

walk far enough away. His days were marked
in varied degrees of suffering, varied
degrees of shame. So when the brilliant youth

stood trembling, waiting in the road ahead,
he felt the weight of his long burden briefly
lift, and when the youth rushed to embrace him,

the leper startled to discern his body
gently held, and held in firm, benevolent
esteem, and when he felt the kiss across

his ruined cheek, he found forgotten light
returning to his eyes, and looked to meet
the brother light approaching from the young man's

beaming face. Each man blessed the other
with this light that then became the way,
thereafter, each would travel every road.

Note

how on occasion
the treble clef turns
triply cleft, troubling

the air imparted
of an evening
to the page. The score

thus parsed amplifies
what polyphony
the ear has lately

apprehended, just
beneath the hearing,
tutoring the hand.

So, every note might
yield its own surround,
intone its own implied

accompaniment,
each note of which might
also launch a layered

orchestration, which
subsequently grants
another measure

yet, and endlessly.
                    —for JAC Redford

In Reference to His Annunciation
—apology for Primo Levi

I am sorry for your ancient
      pain, and for your more
contemporary suffering
      which extends impossibly
beyond my knowing.
      I stand chagrined by the brittle
edge our common history
      has honed upon your vision,
and by the way this long
      and righteous rage has served to chill
certain human sympathies.
      Our wretched circumstance
has left you—not for nothing—
      with so little pleasure
in the pulse of those around you.
      And if these words
bear now a trace of censure,
      forgive me all the more.
I have no agency to apprehend
      the world's appearance
before your burning eyes.
      I am most sorry for the tin
taste of righteousness,
      self-assigned, which can taint
the purest waters, and
      —it would appear—nearly any cup.

Euripides the Athenian
after Seferis

He found old age awaiting him   on a spare and limpid plain
    between Troy's embers and the mines'   tall white plume near Sicily.

He craved damp caves along the shore,   and would fix for hours upon
    complex oils of the sea, that chaos   of light where sea met sky.

Years before, when he first discerned   the fine veins of *anthropos*
    proved nets strung by impassive gods   to gather him, and to bind,
    he'd cut his heart to shreds trying   to escape that ancient craft.

His end? Soured to the core, and blind,   alone. When the Fates were done
    with him, even they turned away,   that he be torn apart by dogs.

147

The Righteous Man of Gomorrah

And when he woke he lay confounded on the plain,
    his body blistered, burnt, encrusted in a husk
        of salt, which crazed and fell from him as he sat up.
Around him all the city lay erased, and he
    sat blinking in a sparkling plain of bitter dust.
    And then the rains began. Their touch upon his flesh

was both exquisite and a searing pain, and woke
    the man more fully to the spanning wreck. He called
        the names of wife and child. Neither merited reply.

And when a sea arrived to glut that blank expanse,
    he named it *Met*—because it bore in tepid depths
        the death of all he cherished—then drank his fill of it.

Icons

As windows go, these ancient
gilded figures both receive
our rapt attention and announce

a subtle reciprocity.
We look to them to apprehend
a glimpse of life enduring

out of time; and likewise find
our own experience attended
by a tranquil gaze that turns

increasingly affectionate,
indulgent, kind. The stuff of them
—the paint, the wood, the lucent

golden nimbi—also speaks
in favor of how good
all *stuff* remains despite our long

held habits of abuse, disinterest,
glib dichotomies dividing
meager views of *body* and its

anima. On his knees, the pilgrim
leans into another mode
of being, leans into the stillness

at the urgent source of life.
On his knees, the pilgrim meets
the painted gaze, and finds his own

sight answering a question
now just coming into view.

No Harbor

What if he *did* attain the long-
desired harbor? What if at last
he came to rest? The stillness

of that projected circumstance
revealed just why his most beloved
theologies would not exactly

·satisfy, why allegory
proved so sure to sink the heart
in shallow waters. The ship

with its unfathomed hold
of dim provisions asked for more
than this. No final harbor, nor

the glib assurance of the pier,
but something inarticulate
and . . . well . . . inexhaustible.

He'd meant to keep things moving,
even so, but found his options
worn a little thin, and tinny

both in tenor and in tone. Terror
sports a patent inconvenience,
true enough, but stands regardless

in an absolutely brighter light
than calm—smug and over-fed.
The dead would surely tell him,

if he'd ask them, that the play
of giddy theater extends
beyond the grave, continues

unabated, unconstrained,
extends beyond the fairest
guess, and well beyond his dream.

In Hope of Recollection

It may not be so much
that *mind* appears so poor
a late translation of
the troubled *nous.* Could be
that what can pass these days
for *mind* among us has
grown so thin, un-bodied.
If thought alone results
from that gray organ's urge
and agency, I'd say
your organism's
fairly screwed, or unfairly,
and you are frankly stuck
with faulty gear. Cheer up,
we've all been there; and look!
it may play out to be
just where we now begin.
I have a hunch our hope
rests yet in moving on,
in acting pilgrim to
another way that might
just lead to something like
reunion with the strewn
self's past constituents.
I had a vision once
of light, or was it heat,
or one brief pulsing stutter
—as a hummingbird
visiting my chest quite near
the heart. You will believe this
or you won't. I thought at first

I was in trouble. Then
I knew I was, but found
that forlorn circumstance
suddenly amenable.
I stopped and stood, leaning in
for what seems now no time
at all, palm to chest, confused
at what it might have been.
The icons on the wall
held still. The vigil light
also held its steady flame.
If I was changed, I couldn't
say exactly how. I'll chance
though, in the interim,
the pulse itself has kept me,
similarly, on certain,
fortunate occasions,
thus mindful, still.

Hidden City

... that you might approach the Jerusalem of the heart ...

—Isaac the Least

And now I think Jerusalem abides untouched,
the temple yet intact, its every cornerstone
in place, its vault replete with vivid scent, its ark

alight with vigil lamps whose oil is never spent.
In psalm the pilgrim asks forgiveness, pleads that God
return the Spirit to the heart, and look, the Ghost

had never left, had never for an instant drawn
away, had only watched His presence made obscure
by soul's own intermittent darkening. Just so,

the three companions of the Lord had blindly walked
the lesser part of three dim years before their eyes
beheld the Light that bathed the Son eternally.

Just so, the Light of Tabor spools extending past
the vision of the multitude, if nonetheless
apparent to the meek, the poor, the pure in heart.

Just so, the Holy City bides within the heart,
awaits the day the pilgrim will arrive, will quit
the road, turn in to greet his City's boundless sweep, and see.

Late Sounding

So much of what the sea has suffered
is laid upon the shore, so much of what
we lose to it returns, dropped into our laps

unrecognizable, ruined or worked to artifact.
The little skiff I rowed until my arms were sore
is by now parsed to glib constituents, broadcast

in a ring around the calm abyss of our modest
Hood Canal. The shore has long proved adequate
to hold the millings of the sea, at least those bits

it doesn't swallow whole. What's left are these
smooth tokens and, with them, a lucent store
of fragments raised from memory's cool vault—

bright mornings pulling at the oars to check the pots,
the race to meet my mother at the pier, and one
long day adrift and waiting for my father to return

from salmon fishing with Hap and Uncle Ray.
To touch those moments now is hard, and made
more difficult with every passing bier, as we

attend our own slow dissolution, worn, and leaning in.

Autopsy

—after Elytis

And look, just beneath the skin, a most challenging stratum
of cedar bark ribbons, overlapping
as if one were thatching a longhouse or hut.

His heart, laid open, revealed a dense island of evergreens and mist.
His entrails had become the stuff of heavy cloud or wood-
smoke maybe, and there, farther down, an alder fire raging.

At the section of one lung, a raven's cry escaped, then
from the other, the gull's complaint. Those who heard this,
began to hasten their grim work. His eyes

that never could quite focus on anything near, continued
with their search, as a shaft of light descending
through storm. Lifting one retina, they found within

a cluttered reliquary—beneath its twin, a vacant tomb.
The ears proved unfathomable, each a salty bay, still
visited by the tide and scuttling, hidden life. When finally they reached

the gray matter packed within, they found a parched desert whose sands
yet gripped the bones of a fallen monk. He appeared
to have failed—and just here—in the very midst of prayer.

Replies to the Immediate

No, he mumbled from the podium, the poems
are not my songs. A breeze
troubled the papers in his hands, and a shift
in the air also sent
a wave across those seated, tossing their hair,
their broad lapels, their scarves.
The programs in their hands also whispered. Nor,
the man continued, nor
are they my prayers. At that word, the air grew still,
and across his face passed both
a tremor and a calm. Song, he said, attains
to a condition the poem
dare not attend. And prayer? Who would frame a poem
when he had better find
his knees, in silence, having put his art away?

Evening Prayer

And what *would* you pray in the troubled midst
of this our circular confusion save
that the cup be taken away? That the chill
and welling of the blood might suffer by His
hushed mercy to abate, to calm the legion
dumb anxieties as each now clamors
to be known and named? The road has taken
on, of late, the mute appearance of a grief
whose leaden gravity both insists on speed
and slows the pilgrim's progress to a crawl.
At least he's found his knees. I bear a dim
suspicion that this circumstance will hold
unyielding hegemony until the day.
What *would* you pray at the approach of this
late evening? What ask? And of whom?

Secret Poem
—after Seferis

Yes. I have seen the end, and yes
I was disturbed by what I saw.
That I yet glimpse occasional
and frankly stirring satisfactions
in the way the paper draws the ink
may prove one mode of consolation.

That I continue to appreciate
a morning walk, an evening's
intercourse should also speak
encouragement, no? The end
appalls. Quite so. Though I wouldn't say
the end appalls more fully

than the interim. The present
situation—electoral
absurdity, real TV, unprovoked
slaughter thoroughly explained—such
assaults attain a state insisting
that the end arrive, and quickly.

The past is ever with us, but most
have pared it to a less demanding
heft, utilitarian. For me, the past
has become lately my own
articulation of that scene
I saw, just now, as very like the end.

September 11

And the pillar of fire, and the pillar of cloud
Did not depart from before the people.
        —*Exodus 13:22*

According to the promise, we had known
we would be led, and that the ancient God
would deign to make His hidden presence shown
by column of fire, and pillar of cloud.

We had come to suspect what fierce demand
our translation to another land might bode,
but had not guessed He would allow our own
brief flesh to bear the flame, become the cloud.

About Paraclete Press
Who We Are
Paraclete Press is an ecumenical publisher of books and recordings on Christian spirituality. Our publishing represents a full expression of Christian belief and practice—from Catholic to Evangelical, from Protestant to Orthodox.

Paraclete Press is the publishing arm of the Community of Jesus, an ecumenical monastic community in the Benedictine tradition. As such, we are uniquely positioned in the marketplace without connection to a large corporation and with informal relationships to many branches and denominations of faith.

We like it best when people buy our books from booksellers, our partners in successfully reaching as wide an audience as possible.

What We Are Doing
Books
Paraclete Press publishes books that show the richness and depth of what it means to be Christian. Although Benedictine spirituality is at the heart of all that we do, we publish books that reflect the Christian experience across many cultures, time periods, and houses of worship.

We publish books that nourish the vibrant life of the church and its people—books about spiritual practice, formation, history, ideas, and customs.

We have several different series of books within Paraclete Press, including the bestselling Living Library series of modernized classic texts; *A Voice from the Monastery*—giving voice to men and women monastics about what it means to live a spiritual life today; award-winning literary faith fiction; and books that explore Judaism and Islam and discover how these faiths inform Christian thought and practice.

Recordings
From Gregorian chant to contemporary American choral works, our music recordings celebrate the richness of sacred choral music through the centuries. Paraclete is proud to distribute the recordings of the internationally acclaimed choir Gloriæ Dei Cantores, who have been praised for their "rapt and fathomless spiritual intensity" by *American Record Guide*, and the Gloriæ Dei Cantores Schola, which specializes in the study and performance of Gregorian chant. Paraclete is also the exclusive North American distributor of the Monastic Choir of St. Peter's Abbey in Solesmes, France, long considered to be a leading authority on Gregorian chant performance.

Learn more about us at our Web site,
www.paracletepress.com
or call us toll-free at
1-800-451-5006.

Other Poetry from Paraclete Press

Deaths and Transfigurations: Poems
Paul Mariani
With Engravings by Barry Moser

94 pages
ISBN: 1-55725-452-4
$24.00, Hardcover

This provocative collection of beautiful poems searches and develops the human themes of personal loss, the quest for new life, and the transfiguring moments that are possible in the mysteries of living.

Barry Moser, one of the world's foremost book designers and illustrators, has created a series of original, integrated engravings corresponding to these major themes in Mariani's verse.

"I can think of no other poet who probes with such passionate, yearning intensity the soul, the psyche, and 'the mansions of old memories.' This is his finest book yet."
—Ron Hansen, author of *Mariette in Ecstasy* and other books

A Pentecost of Finches: New & Selected Poems
Robert Siegel

179 pages
ISBN: 1-55725-430-3
$26.00, Hardcover

"Nothing is unseen or untouched here," the poet Robert Lowell wrote of Robert Siegel's poetry, and it is equally true of these new and selected poems. Moving up the chain of being from inchworm to angel, these poems celebrate *being* in all its aspects, from unsettling glimpses of the abyss to union with nature and that which transcends it. On the way they explore the mystery of evil, the meaning of history, our own mysterious quests, and the human search for transformative joy.

"Of Robert Siegel's talents there can be no doubt. . . . His poems are a power."
—Joseph Parisi, in *Poetry*

Available from most booksellers or through Paraclete Press:
www.paracletepress.com; 1-800-451-5006.
Try your local bookstore first.